Teachers' Companion & Coach

SMILING CHALK

AF148823

Karamjeet Singh

Aditi Bhasin

New Delhi | 2023

First Edition
2023
ISBN: 000-00-000000-0-0
© www.smilingchalk.com

ABOUT SMILING CHALK

This raised a few vital questions, like who are happy teachers? What goes in a happy classroom? What are the tools and techniques used by happy teachers? Is it possible for anyone to emulate the best practices and bring the same magic in their classrooms? How to empower teachers to bring joy into their classrooms? How could we help our teachers to increase their self-awareness and happiness quotient? Could there be a blueprint of creating happy, harmonious, and hallowed classrooms?

FOR FURTHER INFORMATION

Karamjeet Singh Sodhi
Q 552 Rishi Nagar Rani Bagh
New Delhi - 110034
9899907787
Smilingchalk@gmail.com

SMILING CHALK
Karamjeet Singh & Aditi Bhasin

COVER & LAYOUT
Dayaram Lohia
Dayaram Lohia Creative Studio Service
New Delhi

Creative Head, Fusion Arts Foundation

HAPPINESS,
ENGAGEMENT,
AWARENESS,
RESOURCES &
TRANSFORMATION

FOREWORD

मनीष सिसोदिया
MANISH SISODIA

उप मुख्यमंत्री, दिल्ली सरकार
दिल्ली सचिवालय, आई.पी. एस्टेट,
नई दिल्ली—110002

Deputy Chief Minister, GNCTD
Delhi Secretariat, I.P. Estate,
New Delhi-110002

Visions are like plants that need to be nurtured with patience and persistence not by a single person but by a dedicated team.

When the Government led by Chief Minister Shri. Arvind Kejriwal took charge to reform the education system in Delhi, we envisioned an educational model where teachers are passionate about teaching, learners are excited to learn, and parents are proud of sending their wards to government schools. To turn this dream into reality, we started with some sincere and dedicated teachers who would breathe life in the schools. The magic soon began. Principals turned into dynamic leaders and teachers into facilitators. 21st-century skills and happiness are now an integral part of the school culture. Teachers are collaborating, taking initiative, and inspiring their younger generation to set new benchmarks for themselves.

Smiling Chalk is one such initiative taken by two distinguished teachers of the Delhi Government schools- Karamjeet Singh & Aditi Bhasin.

The book, Smiling Chalk is highly informative for teachers. The acronym, H.E.A.R.T that deals with five major aspects of a happy classroom brought a smile on my face. The authors have provided a comprehensive compendium of strategies and ideas that can help every teacher to infuse new energy in the classroom, irrespective of the content or context.

I hope "Smiling Chalk" will inspire teachers to take more and more initiatives and work in harmony to create resources and references for their other colleagues and learners. Through this book, I would like to appeal to teachers and educators to develop the practice of recording, replicating, and propagating their learnings for their colleagues. This book will certainly create a dynamic culture that will further inspire the education community to create new and progressive learning opportunities for our children.

Congratulations to the authors for their maiden endeavour!

Manish Sisodia

INTRODUCTION

What Palmer has shared in his article, "Heart of a Teacher", is in complete agreement with what we have observed, experienced, and taught in our teaching and mentoring tenure. The essence of Palmer's essay is, we teach who we are and our classroom environment is the outward projection of our inner environment. Knowingly or unknowingly our mental makeup is brushed on our students in the classroom. It triggered a thought in us, that a happy teacher is the one who can create a happy classroom.

This raised a few vital questions, like who are happy teachers? What goes in a happy classroom? What are the tools and techniques used by happy teachers? Is it possible for anyone to emulate the best practices and bring magic in their classrooms? How to empower teachers to bring joy into their classrooms? How could we help our teachers to increase their self-awareness and happiness quotient? Could there be a blueprint of creating happy, harmonious, and hallowed classrooms?

Our inquest probed us for breaching the normal way of seeking answers and verbally guiding the teachers. We thought of interviewing happy teachers and exemplary veterans, penning down their sharing and compiling our key learnings and observations in the form of a book, Smiling Chalk. It is a compendium of proven, practised, and observed classroom interventions that can create and sustain a culture of joyful teaching & learning across content or context.

It encapsulates decades of our first-hand experiences with a wide spectrum of school education, classroom teaching, teacher training, observations and curriculum development. It has the longest and closest observational experiences gathered at the grass root level of a revolutionary education model, the education model of Delhi government. Smiling Chalk is

"I am a teacher at heart, and there are moments in the classroom when I can hardly hold the joy. When my students and I discover uncharted territory to explore, when the pathway out of a thicket opens up before us, when our experience is illumined by the lightning-life of the mind then teaching is the finest work I know."
— **Parker J Palmer**, Heart of a Teacher

To create happy classrooms, the primary ingredient is a happy and positive teacher. Such teachers are usually resilient and capable of dealing with stress irrespective of the stressors around. They take pleasure in teaching and hardly miss any chance to create and cherish happiness in their class. They understand and emulate **Happiness** within and around, know ways and means to **Engage** their learners, are well Aware of their learners, adept at creating and managing **Resources**, and well equipped with tools to **Transform** the classroom culture according to the need of content and context.

When all these elements work together, they help teachers create a positive environment of purpose, potential and possibilities. As these elements encompass almost every aspect of any teaching- learning process thus, they work as the heart of a happy classroom. Each chapter elaborates on each aspect of **H.E.A.R.T**, i.e.,
Happiness, Engagement, Awareness, Resources & Transformation.

enriched with diversified knowledge gained through multiple exposures to distinguished schools and institutions both at national and international level.

HAPPINESS,
ENGAGEMENT,
AWARENESS,
RESOURCES &
TRANSFORMATION

Experiences, Exposures and Experiments with Education for more than two decades including 06 years of mentorship with Delhi Government has given us the confidence and the wisdom to locate some of the common principles of productive teaching-learning process in a classroom and gather tools for not just efficient but effective teaching.

One of the most common attributes of any productive classroom that we could find was the overall happiness index of the teachers and their unique ways to make their learners feel valued and connected. A teacher learner relation as we understood can be summed up as

"Learners will forget what you taught, they will also forget the marks you gave, but they will never forget how you made them feel."

Blessed and happy are the teachers who aspire to bring happiness in their classrooms, they are the ones with positive mental attitude, they are inquisitive to know their learners and ensure that their learners know that they are known, they know the importance and ways of sharpening their axe and managing their resources, they are willing and competent of creating a culture of gratitude, respect, recognition and appreciation, they successfully engage themselves and their learners in small and large groups for collaborative learning, they are resourceful and above all they are happy.

Smiling Chalk is woven around a core belief, that, emulating and implementing the steps and strategies of happy teachers can help other willing teachers for creating and sustaining a similar happy classroom in their context. Each chapter is fully equipped with insights and interesting activities which may help teachers to transform their classroom into a happy classroom from a dull, boring, and monotonous classroom. Smiling Chalk can be seen as a blueprint of positive mindset habits and practices followed by teachers all across the globe. Whether you are a classroom teacher, a trainer, a coach or a facilitator, you will find this book as a companion by your side always ready to offer you solutions to transform your classroom environment.

We consider ourselves as happy teachers and trainers, with happy and positive spirits we hand you over our experience, exposures and efforts in this form of a book with a pristine hope that you will receive and use the book in the same spirit in which it was written and compiled.

Smiling Chalk is our special way to express our gratitude, pride and joy of being a teacher, just a teacher, not any superhero with a cape and magical powers but simple human beings with human touch unaware of the lives they have touched, they are touching, and waiting to be touched. It celebrates teachers and salutes their never dying spirit of always standing up for their learners and making them feel valued and empowered.

With Happy Hopes!!

— Karamjeet Singh
— Aditi Bhasin

ACKNOWLEDGEMENTS

W hen Aditi & I conceptualized the idea of collating our learnings and training in the form of a book, we were quite skeptical about the idea. Although we had decades of teaching experience, writing a book was altogether a new dimension. It was through the unconditional support of our near ones and a deep mutual trust in each other that we could take the initiative, and finally, the book, "**Smiling Chalk**", is in your hand. It fills our hearts with ecstasy and gratitude to recall the learnings and contributions of all the extraordinary teachers, educationists, and visionaries whom we have met, interviewed and referred to for this book. There are, as they say, far too many to thank individually. Nonetheless, we do need to thank some specific people who had a direct hand in bringing this book into reality.

First, we would like to thank exemplary educators who spared their valuable time and shared their practical wisdom about happy teaching and joyful learning with us. To begin with, the Education Minister of Delhi, Mr. Manish Sisodia, who shared his inputs about happiness and the changing roles of teachers in the 21st century, Mr. Himanshu Gupta, IAS (Director Education, Delhi) , Mr. Shailender Sharma (Principal Advisor to Director Education, Delhi), and Dr. B.P. Pandey (OSD, School Branch) Dr. Sunil Kumar Arora HOS (GCSV Rampura) for encouraging and guiding us. We acknowledge all the valuable inputs and insights shared by Ms. Mamta Saikia, CEO Bharti Foundation. Her rich and diversified experiences with classroom cultures of recognition and appreciations are vital for this book. We also feel thankful to Ms. Geeta Mishra (District Coordinator happiness, Delhi) for her valuable inputs on happiness and its various classroom aspects.

Next, we would like to extend our gratitude to all those organizations, teachers and authors whose ideas and strategies we have shared in our book. This book is the outcome of exposures, training and resources we have earned through esteemed organizations like SCERT Delhi, Directorate of Education, Delhi, Regional English Language Office, the US Embassy, TESOL, NIE (Singapore), British Council, global universities etc., which we have given in the book as tools for transformative and effective teaching. Some of the key learnings of the book are derived and inspired from our online interactive series, "*Smiling Chalk Laughing Duster*" that hosted national and international awardees from different parts of India and world to discuss about "*Happy Teachers and Happy Classrooms.*"

We are grateful to all of our distinguished guests for openly sharing the initiatives and interventions they have been using to bring joy into their schools and classrooms.

ACKNOWLEDGEMENTS

Mr. Tapeshwar Jugran, Ms. Manu Gulati and Ms. Neeru Lohiya from Delhi; Mr. Harinder Grewal, Mr. Amarjit Singh, Mr. Luvjeet Grewal, and Mr. Kirandeep Tiwana from Punjab; Mr. Sarvesht Mishra and Ms. Snehil Pandey from Uttar Pradesh; Dr. Shaila from Bengaluru; Dr. Mir from Jammu Kashmir; Mr. Lomas Dhungel from Sikkim, Mr. Rakesh from Gujrat; Mr. Kalayan Mankoti from Almora, Ms. Maria Barouta from Greece, and Mr. Jan Aldrin C. Belsario from Philippines, are some of the awardees featured on our series. Their sharings have been pivotal for the content and concept development of the book.

We feel indebted to our editor and designer Mr. Dayaram Lohia from Fusion Art Foundation for his dedicated efforts and relentless spirit for excellence. Without him it would not have been possible to bring this book into its present form. We are also thankful to Ms. Megha Narula for her valuable contributions in the initial designing and editing of the book.

Unconditional love and blessings of our parents and close friends have been our consistent source of strength and motivation. Aditi's daughter Arushi and my niece Reet were our source of creative inputs and critical reviews. They have pressed us to be clearer and sharper in our content presentation.

Last but not the least we are indebted to the Almighty for choosing us for this noble purpose and look forward to more such opportunities to learn, serve, and share.

With Immense Gratitude!!

Karamjeet Singh

Aditi Bhasin

PREFACE

For ages, there have been different kinds of schools and classrooms, and each classroom has a primary objective to trigger learning, although impact and efficacy differs. Classrooms are defined by the environment they carry, like a disciplined classroom will have discipline as the top priority. Similarly, there are engaging classrooms, distracted classrooms, uncontrollable classrooms, activity-based classrooms, digital classrooms, and so many others. Still, out of all these classrooms, there is this one kind of classroom that has always proved to be the most engaging, enriching, and enjoyable one, and that is a "Happy Classroom".

To simply state, a happy classroom is the one where teachers, learners, and classrooms are all happy and positive. They are happy interacting with each other; they are happy doing activities; they are happy while learning; they are happy being assessed and just happy all the time. Being happy, they are more creative and enthusiastic. They are not afraid of facing challenges and are ready to embrace opportunities to lead, perform and support. Within these vibrant classrooms, both teachers and learners are happy to teach and learn, share and care, ask and tell or give and receive.

These are the classrooms where students feel psychologically safe and participate with zeal and enthusiasm. These are the classrooms that follow the principal policy of NCLB, i.e. No Child Left Behind. These are all-inclusive classrooms where everyone is happy, including the chalk, the walls, and the duster. The common underlying element of these truly progressive and productive classrooms is happiness.

These are the classrooms where you not only see happy teachers and blooming kids, but you may also find some smiling chalks and a few laughing dusters. In such spaces, one experiences high levels of communication, collaboration, and creativity. A natural question that pops up in the mind, Is it possible to create such happy and positive classrooms?

The answer is YES!

By emulating and implementing the steps and strategies of teachers and educationists who have been able to create such classrooms in their contexts. From principles of learning to practically implemented strategies, from budding pre-service teachers to experienced in-service teachers, from classroom teaching to classroom observations, and from first-hand experiences to interviews of exemplary teachers, we have gathered some critical learnings and wisdom to locate a few common yet core principles of effective teaching and learning.

Each core factor is then elaborated upon and supported with illustrations in the form of a lesson. The intent is to make teachers aware and help them imbibe these principles to make their classrooms equally effective and happy as those of happy teachers.

Within each chapter, you will get some proven strategies, tips and tricks to make your classrooms happy. These are the positive mindset habits and practices followed by teachers all across the globe to make their classroom environment positive, productive, and progressive. All the activities and resources shared in the book are proven and implementable. Each topic has been researched, designed, and presented in a way that you will find fun and joy in adapting to your own context and classroom. We hand over our experiences, exposures and efforts to you in the form of this book with a pristine hope that you will receive and use the book in the same spirit in which it was written and compiled. Before you begin your journey towards happy classrooms, just remember and keep this thought with you throughout the journey,

You are doing a good job!

Now you have ideas and tools to do it better.

CONTENTS

1

HAPPINESS
WITHIN AND AROUND

> *Students don't need a perfect teacher, all that they need is a happy teacher. Who is going to make them excited to come to school and develop a love for learning*

We teachers spend a great deal of time in our classrooms. If this much quantity of time would lack quality and positivity it might become a prominent stressor for us. We need welcoming and uplifting classrooms that rejuvenate us rather than drain us. Most of us must have felt , that, stress and burnouts stems out of monotonous teaching routines and never ending administrative tasks. We may feel proud that we are in a noble profession. We help our learners to discover their purpose and potential, but with a stressed mindset we fail to create conducive classrooms for such noble endeavours.

Kothari Commission (1964) one of the most significant Indian Education Commission quotes, "*Destiny of a nation is shaped by its curriculum*", and it is true. The values, skills, and knowledge acquired in classrooms play a pivotal role in shaping responsible and competent citizens.

Classrooms that provide positive reinforcement to learners pave a path for a progressive nation. Such positive and progressive classrooms are paramount if we want to influence our nation's destiny positively. Schools and universities should be training grounds for students to develop a love for their country, passion for their work, and compassion for each other as fellow citizens.

If the destiny is shaped by the curriculum, then classrooms are those studios and we teachers are the sculptors. As a matter of fact,

> *"Engineers build buildings, artists paint paintings Doctors treat patients, but teachers make them all."*

Just like an artist needs a studio and a scientist needs a laboratory, we teachers also need classrooms that are happy and productive. Classrooms, where we are eager to teach and students are excited to learn. Where happiness happens naturally and learners feel a deep connection with us. Where challenges are seen as opportunities and obstacles as stepping ladders. Where we are equipped with resources and our learners feel enriched. Where learners are valued over learnings and well-being matters more than well doings. Where teaching is joyful and learning is cheerful. Where no one is left out and everything goes right in the hearts of teachers and learners.

At the core of a positive learning environment is a happy classroom,
and at the core of a happy classroom is a happy teacher.

Who is a Happy Teacher?

Happy teachers are successful teachers, they find joy and contentment in teaching. They love to be in the classrooms with their learners. They are not only well equipped with methods and strategies but also have that humanly touch of love, care, and mutual respect. They are successful because they take pride and privilege in changing the world. Earl Nightingale defined success as the progressive realisation of a worthy ideal.Teachers who have this worthy ideal to bring smiles on the faces of tiny toddlers are surely the happy and successful teachers. This is what they ever wanted to be, happy teachers, spreading cheers all around and inspiring all those learners who come into their contact.

One of the renowned Educationists Sir Ken Robinson, PhD. in one of his books, "*Creative Schools*", envisions education as a living process just like agriculture and compares a teacher to a gardener. In the words of Sir Ken Robinson, *"Gardner knows they don't make plants grow. They don't attach the roots, glue the leaves, and paint the petals. Plants grow themselves. The gardener's job is to create the best conditions for that to happen. Good gardeners create those conditions, and poor ones don't. It is the same with teaching. Good teachers create the conditions for learning, and poor ones don't. Good teachers also know that they are not always in control of these conditions."* (Ken Robinson & Lou Aronica,2016; *Creative Schools*; Penguin Books, PP 102).

Parker J Palmer, a famous linguist and educationist, once quoted, *"Whoever our students may be, whatever the subject we teach, ultimately we teach who we are."* In other words, the environment of any classroom is actually the expanded reflection of the teacher's state of mind. In short,

*"Stressed teachers create stressed classrooms,
and happy teachers create happy classrooms."*

Happy teachers are not necessarily stress free teachers but they are the teachers with a positive mental attitude. PMA or positive mental attitude for teachers is a foundation on which happy classrooms are constructed. Teachers with PMA have complete control over their classroom choices and activities. They are always brimming with energy and enthusiasm.

Positive Mental Attitude (PMA) for Teachers

A Positive Mental Attitude is best described by Napoleon Hill as an ability to recognize seeds of equal or greater benefits in every adversity, every failure and every heartache.

Despite thousands of failures, Sir Thomas Alva Edison's Positive Mental Attitude was the only thing that kept him going for the discovery of the light bulb. PMA was the only thing that allowed the Wright Brothers to make flying possible and helped Anne Frank pen down her journey to inspire the world. This positive attitude only gave Anne Sullivan the courage and perseverance to nurture and illuminate her student, Hellen Keller-the legendary reformist. Throughout human history, there are countless examples of triumphs over impossibilities only through a PMA. Leaders, scientists, industrialists, teachers, etc., like Gandhi, Martin Luther King Jr., Abraham Lincoln, Benjamin Franklin, Anne Sullivan, Stephen Hawking, Victor E. Frankl, Harrison Ford, and Madam Curie are some of those who had that positive mindset to keep their eyes on solutions and possibilities rather than on problems and difficulties.

A few years back, in a workshop with a group of teachers on Classroom Management, we opened the workshop with a question, *"In your opinion, what is a teacher's most important role in a learners' life?"* Out of all the interesting and insightful responses, one unusual reply came from a veteran teacher. She responded in a firm voice, *"For me, it would be to ensure that no stone has been left unturned."* It was an unusual reply, so we nudged her to elaborate it a little further. What she responded has stayed with us as a lesson for life.

She started by replying with a famous quote by Swami Vivekananda, *"Education is the manifestation of the perfection already in man."* She continued, *"I strongly believe in it; thus, being a teacher, my only quest has been to look out for those seeds of passion and perfection in my students. "*

After a brief pause, she continued, *"My fundamental role as a teacher has been to look under the stones to search for hidden talents & untapped potential areas of learners to help them manifest their true purpose and potential. "*

It takes a lot of patience and perseverance to discover all the possible possibilities; a learner might seem interested in one area and might fail to pursue it for a long time. Only passionate teachers keep searching for the interest areas of children till they find the clarity and definiteness in their interests and purpose.

During this process of relentless searching, tapping, and de-covering of hidden talents, the teacher meets obstacles and frustrations. Only the resilient ones keep pursuing their objective. After many piles of ignorance and catacombs of the prescribed curriculum have been uncovered, the true purpose and potential of the learner emerge.

The moment she stopped sharing, there was a massive round of applause in the hall.

On that day, we received the core purpose of teaching i.e., to help our learners to discover their hidden potential. Our quest from that day onwards was to observe the process of seeking and breaking that process into doable steps. So that teachers, irrespective of the context, may trigger the journey to bring out the latent talents of their learners. We learnt the significance of trust and mutual respect as pillars on which happy classrooms are build.

TRUST - The Foundational Step

Whether it's life in general or of any specific endeavour, the process begins with trust, which Merriam-Webster defines as assured reliance on the character, ability, strength, or truth of someone or something. There's a famous saying, "Trust the process", but it seems like a limited vision of the word "Trust", as it is not just the process where trust is needed. A true approach to understand trust is to see it as a tripolar phenomenon,

- The first pole would be the teacher's trust in herself and her potential to help his/her pupil. it is also called as self-efficacy or teacher efficacy.

- Second, she must have trust in the hidden potential of each learner sitting in the classroom.

- Third and the last is the deep trust in the process.

A strong trust in one's instincts and a confident conviction in an individual's hidden potential are the beginning coordinates of the journey towards discovering latent talents.

Just like Anne Sullivan's PMA enabled Hellen Keller to tap all her possibilities and achieve her highest potential, we teachers trigger the process by providing a wide range of Opportunities, Exposure, Environment, and Education to the learners.

Teachers observe the interest areas of the children and, whenever the teacher finds excitement and readiness in learners, she provides resources and opportunities to learn, try, fail, stumble, and triumph.

Once the teacher finds that the appropriate time has been given, she tries to ascertain the passion and understanding of the learner towards the chosen area through a test.

With test scores, the teacher now provides opportunities and platforms for training the learners in their chosen field of interest.

The teacher then tracks the learners' willingness and competencies through the training and post- training period till the learners triumph over their quest to pursue the field of his/her passion and potential.

This mental attitude and clarity in the process enabled Mr. Sonam Wangchuk to transform the lives of school dropouts at his exemplary school situated in Leh, the remotest corner of India with extreme climatic conditions. Students at his centre learn innovations and technology and design their future paths through trials and training.

Teachers with PMA are always happier and look out for opportunities to help their learners to discover and pursue their purpose and passion areas with persistence and perseverance.

PMA in Action

Rewards of PMA and the connection established with students are not instantaneous but are felt when they look up to us and cherish the moments they had spent with us. Ms. Geeta Mishra, an experienced teacher and Happiness Coordinator with Government schools of Delhi, happily recalls and shares one such incident of care and connect that, one morning, while she was strolling in the lawns of her society, she was called by a sweet yet firm voice from behind her back. When she turned back there was this young girl smiling with tears of joy. On coming closer, Geeta realised that this young and dynamic girl had once been a shy and under-confident student of her class about 10 years ago. She asked the girl if she was Anjali. And the mixed emotions that Anjali felt were one of its kind. *"Ma'am, I am so lucky that you remember my name even though you taught me 8 years ago. I can never forget a kind and concerned teacher like you. You worked like a catalyst to transform my life. There was a time when I was on the verge of quitting school. But you kept my confidence high and even helped me after school with my weak areas. Even my parents felt that I should drop out from school but you had rock-solid confidence in me. You are even more caring than my own mother. And not just that but you remember me, even years after of not being in physical contact with me."* This constant assurance of the teacher with PMA transformed this shy girl into an independent and confident pathologist.

Going That Extra Mile

The fundamental desire of every human is to be happy. Happiness is no where or happiness is now here. We have to understand that happiness is here and now, it is not found anywhere outside but deep within us and we are the creators of our destiny. The level of happiness reaches its optimum when we feel we have found our purpose and passion in life and

Geeta Mishra sincerely believes,

"The purpose of education is not merely teaching academic subjects to learners, but also developing their inherent capabilities, polishing them, making the learner realise his/her true potential and enable his/her walk towards becoming self-reliant. There have been times when the love and passion of the teacher makes him/her believe that their learners can achieve much more than what they presently have. And for this, only a teacher, who has found her purpose can help her learners also identify and unleash theirs. All this would be possible if a stimulating learning environment is created and the most precious resource, that is our time, is given to all, even to the last child in the class."

when we align ourselves with the undisputed fact that there is abundance everywhere in the universe and we harness only a very small fraction of it. This will provide us with a directional approach.

If teachers in our classrooms are content and feel they have been chosen to be here with the students, they will understand the fact that they can act as change-makers and undisputed role models for their students.

Going the extra mile is one of the five core success principles recommended by Mr. Napoleon Hill in his book "*Laws of Success.*" We, teachers, are blessed with this divine purpose to understand our pupils and bring a change in their lives.

Assistant lecturer (Physics) Rahul S Chatterjee, the only teacher selected from Meghalaya for the National Teachers Awards 2020 during his interview with Princess Giri Rashir, narrates an incident that changed his role as a teacher. Chatterjee always believed that the role of the teacher wasn't just teaching but much more. He is among those teachers who proceed with a positive mental attitude, and nothing deters them from going some extra miles for their learners.

While narrating the incident, Chatterjee shared, *"A new batch of class eleven had joined. I had given them ten days to get their textbooks and come to class. So that particular day arrived, and students were made to leave the class who did not have textbooks. Three boys and one girl stood up to leave the classroom; while the girl was leaving, she looked up at me and whispered something I didn't pick up. I asked her to come back and repeat what she said. So, the girl said my father isn't at home and I don't have money to buy books,"* narrated Chatterjee.

Struck by the girl's situation and reminded of his own old days, Chatterjee immediately took it up to the Principal and ensured that books were bought for the students at any cost.

"I had a very cooperative Principal. Lots of things were possible because of the cooperation of higher-ups. I started with five books, four were given to the students, and the spare one was kept as a reserve. Next year the word spread; we needed ten books, and the same was done. Now I have 12 books, but in between, the syllabus changed twice or thrice, and with the old books not valid anymore, we had to buy new sets of books. It was then decided that we have a book bank. We provide these books to the children to be used for the entire year to be returned only after the exams just before we gave away the mark sheet," said Chatterjee.

The girl whom Chatterjee had almost thrown out of class for not having a textbook later did excellently well in her exams. In one of the subjects, she even scored the highest marks in the Board Examinations.

Chatterjee said that a little bit of encouragement, when given to the students, always pays back.

"So, these were huge lessons for me. And these were the initial years of my teaching career. It gave me direction; it gave me this thought process that you start doing something for the children, and it will simply come back. That has been my motto throughout these teaching years," said Chatterjee.

Just like Chatterjee, in every school throughout the globe, some teachers take extra pains. Most of the time, efforts go unnoticed. Still, they are happy because efforts might get unnoticed and unrecognised, but they are not wasted. Visible changes in learners' behaviour and performance are the awards that a happy and positive teacher expects the most in return for the extra initiatives. In the long run, teachers who create opportunities for their learners remain close to the hearts of their learners.

Sometimes our small acts of kindness and caring attitude towards our learners are all they need to bring a significant shift in their life. Teachers themselves are clueless about the number of lives they have changed through their kind words and encouraging pats on the back of their learners. However, the learner who gets transformed never forgets those teachers and always cherishes and recalls them with pride and a smile. The objective of teachers like Geeta Mishra or Mr. Chatterjee isn't simply to transmit curriculum but to inspire their learners with hope, self-confidence, and self-reliance. They empower their learners by believing in them, putting in extra effort and helping them identify and nurture seeds of excellence. And you will find these teachers doing every bit with a smile and a mental attitude that is positive, progressive, and productive.

CLASSROOM HAPPINESS: Within and Around

"Happiness is like a flower; it blooms from within and spreads outwards."

Teachers with better conceptual clarity of happiness are more likely to have more ideas and insights to incorporate the elements of happiness in their classrooms. They are familiar with the model of happiness; thus, they are able to create a culture of sustainable happiness in their classrooms. With increasing awareness and the significance of individual happiness for the nation's overall prosperity, India has inspired various other countries and states to make happiness an indispensable part of the school curriculum. When asked about the objectives and impact of introducing the Happiness Curriculum as a new subject for all the students from pre-primary to class 8th, Mr. Manish Sisodia, Deputy Chief Minister & Education Minister, Delhi Government, quotes:

We have scientifically designed a course which helps children focus their attention on the present moment. It enables them to live harmoniously with family and society and is likely to support them in developing a holistic outlook and perspective of life."

He further explains the happiness in classrooms and its role in shaping the desired culture in the classroom and citizenship in our students.

"...the classroom is an open and non-judgmental space for students to deeply engage with oneself and others...these classes are platforms for teachers and students to gain a better understanding of each other through the process of mindful listening and acknowledgement, which will ultimately help build a healthy and harmonious relationship.

Happiness has been the subject of study since ages. But for last few decades it has been studied and researched extensively both scientifically and psychologically. Happiness is no longer a lofty vision but a mainstream subject to be learnt, taught, and practiced. In year 2018, Delhi Government launched and implemented the Happiness Curriculum for classes nursery to 8th. The curriculum has been developed on the model proposed by A Nagraj of Madyastha Darshan. He proposed a model for existence, where he addresses the four dimensions of human living as an integrated form of the material, behavioural, intellectual & experiential aspects. These correspond to our senses, feelings, learning (understanding) & awareness.

Educators, psychologists, and mindfulness experts worked together to create the Happiness Curriculum framework that is now used as a social, and emotional learning program for pre-primary to elementary classes. The idea for the curriculum was laid out by the Deputy Chief Minister of Delhi, Mr. Manish Sisodia, who is the Education Minister as well. The curriculum is based on the "*Happiness Triad*" concept of philosopher A. Nagraj ji. Since 2018 it is running successfully in government schools of Delhi to bring, maintain, and sustain happiness in the classroom. Not only students but teachers have also started adopting mindfulness and virtue based living in their life to bring mental peace and happiness. The Triad of happiness offers the simplest approach to understand and implement happiness both in life and classrooms.

TRIAD OF HAPPINESS

Happiness is the ultimate aim, and we can experience it, explore it and express it in three major ways, viz;

Through Senses, through Emotions and through Meaning. Based on this, the major aspects or elements of happiness can be seen as:

- Sensory Happiness

- Deeper Happiness

- Sustainable Happiness

The concept and brief theory of happiness with illustration is necessary to form the foundational understanding of happiness. On practical grounds it is the mindfulness practice that brings transformation over the period of regular practice.

Sensory Happiness - Through Senses

Happiness felt through the senses is pleasurable but short-lived. For example, the very thought of eating pizza brings water into my mouth, and I feel happy while eating it. But this happiness stays with me only for as long as I am eating or having access to that pizza. What happens when the pizza is gone? It takes along with it, its pleasure and the momentary happiness it provides.

In a classroom, it can be seen as the pleasure and happiness sought by learners and teachers through celebrations, audio-visual interventions, get togethers, field trips, and all those experiences which involve any or all the five senses. Though happiness is episodic, it still plays a vital role in keeping the environment happy and positive.

To quote an example, Yasmeen is a primary teacher who is enthusiastic and happy. One can spot her smiling or laughing at any moment of the day, especially when she is with her learners. She teaches 5th-class students, and the group of learners she teaches has been with her for the last 05 years; her bonding with her learners is strong. It seems like a family of 34 people, with one head of the family and the rest being the kids. When asked about the secret recipe of such strong family-like bonding, she replies, "It is not just the time or the moments we spent together, but the things and the activities we do together. Our favourite and most enjoyable activity since class 1st to 5th has been the "Pot-Luck" activity in which each one of us brings a dish from their home according to the plan, and then all of us cherish the food together. We do it once at the onset of a session and another just before the autumn break. This activity strengthens our bond and creates a feeling of fraternity and belongingness. It helps us to grow acceptance, tolerance, understanding, and mutual appreciation." Such activities, as adopted by Yasmeen, not only help to create episodes of happiness and togetherness but also promote intercultural awareness and understanding.

Deeper Happiness - Through Emotions

A deeper level of happiness is derived from respect, value, love, cooperation, collaboration, and trust.

In our personal lives, we feel happy with our family or friends. We unconditionally give and receive love, care, respect, and other attributes. This happiness is not only deeper but stronger too. It stays longer, but it has its limitations. If sensory happiness is fragile, then more profound happiness is brittle. Relations without trust and understanding fail to survive and die out, leaving some bitter or sour memories, thus hijacking an individual's happiness.

In a classroom, it can be seen and felt in a teachers' relationship with learners and learners with learners. The culture of mutual respect, recognition, and belongingness creates the perfect ground for deeper happiness to grow. The teacher and the learner know the basic tenets of harmonious relationships and treat each tenet as a building block of a happy and collaborative classroom.

A number of schools in Kerala, India, have adopted several strategies to build a deeper level of connection, understanding, and happiness. They celebrate Kindness week, Gratitude

Week and also organise Community Projects, Intercultural Interactions, Nature Walk, etc., to reinforce the strength of the bond between the organisation and the community.

Sustainable Happiness - Through Meaning

Teachers who understand the real meaning of happiness are more likely to transform their classroom culture. By integrating simple and pleasurable activities inside and outside the classroom, they not only provide sensory pleasure but also ensure deeper happiness with recognition, acknowledgement, respect, and care. Students benefit from teachers who go the extra mile to help them transform sensory and deeper happiness into sustainable form.

If we spotlight the lives of legendaries such as Mother Teresa and Mahatma Gandhi, they always had a strong purpose in their lives. This deep-rooted purpose made them happy and positive not for days and weeks but throughout their life. That is what is meant by sustainable happiness.

In a classroom, it can be seen as an attempt to align the Teaching-Learning process with the learning outcomes, the learners with the vision and the mission statement of the school, and help learners to discover their true purpose and potential. One of the effective ways to make all the stakeholders aware and align with the vision and mission statement is through songs and jingles.

And now, the song is sung and performed by students and teachers proudly and subconsciously. All are aligned with the vision and mission statement, thus deriving a sense of common purpose and progress. The song launched by the ministry can be accessed on YouTube by searching for the keyword *"Delhi Shiksha Geet!"*

The true purpose of classroom happiness is to make our learners understand the value of inner peace and experience the power of mindfulness. While describing mindfulness as a *"gift"* given by India to the world in the field of emotional science, the Education Minister of Delhi, Mr. Manish Sisodia, claimed the Happiness Curriculum to be a *"massive success."* He proudly exclaimed that 16 lakh children in Delhi schools start their day with mindfulness every day. The Happiness Curriculum, launched in July 2018, was brought with a vision to strengthen the foundation of happiness and well-being for all students from kindergarten to class 8 in more than a thousand government schools in the national capital of India.

"Mindfulness is the cornerstone of the Happiness Curriculum, and its biggest beauty is that every day lakhs of children in Delhi start their day with mindfulness. It has become a turning point in the lives of students studying in Delhi schools. It has relieved children from stress and increased their focus on studies," Sisodia said during the *"Mindful Education Awards 2021"* program.

"And in fulfilling this dream and making mindfulness a mass movement, the school children will play the role of ambassadors and messengers of mindfulness," a statement quoting Sisodia said.

The *"Mindful Education Awards 2021"* is an initiative to recognize, support, and honour the schools' efforts to create a mentally and physically healthy environment for the growth and development of children.

Many teachers and parents have reported the pupils' interest in academics, and their behaviour has improved because of the curriculum.

The report developed in collaboration with Brookings Institution and Dream a Dream reflects:

- **Impact on Students:** A better relationship with teachers, increased participation inside the classroom and increased focus among students.

- **Impact on Teachers:** Prioritizes values over academic success, changing teaching orientation, and increased collaboration among teachers.

Happiness is the most significant human expression. It can be said that the ultimate aim of all human beings is to achieve happiness in their lives. Across the world, education administrators realise the need for happiness or well-being lessons for children. Self-aware, sensitive, and emotionally mature children are far more successful owing to their advanced ability to engage in meaningful relationships.

The learning outcomes of the Happiness Curriculum are:

- Awareness and focus

- Critical thinking and reflection

- Social-emotional skills

- Confident and pleasant personality

Students who have been with this curriculum proudly share stories of their transformation. One such unforgettable incident was shared by a girl who said the happiness classes had helped her cope with her mother's strife at home because she was a girl. She told us that her brother attended a private school while she attended a government one. Moreover, she often stewed with resentment because of the favouritism shown to her brother at the breakfast table. Since the time happiness classes started, she has been able to leave her resentment behind in the very first period. It helps her focus on her studies. Sadly, this discrimination is happening even in the country's capital. Still, it brings joy to know that the Happiness Classes bring some respite.

While discussing mindfulness in the classroom, Mr. Sisodia remarks:

"With experience, children start to analyse their thoughts. They realise that their thoughts are based on wrong doing in the past, struggles in the present, or concerns about the future. Children are trained not to analyse their thoughts but to focus on how they enter their minds and leave on their own. Slowly but surely, students learn to focus on sounds around them, the working of their bodies, and the thoughts entering and leaving their minds."

Regular and guided mindfulness practice unfolds the multi fold benefits for learners and the overall classroom environment. It has varied benefits for students and they have been observed practically in the lives of students studying in government schools of Delhi. Some of these have been listed below.

Benefits of Mindfulness Exercises

- It helps keeping the focus on studies.

- It helps the students to listen to the teacher carefully.

- While studying at school or home, it helps in maintaining focus.

- It improves retention power and memory.

- It helps in focusing on any activity we are doing right now.

- It helps in being aware of our surroundings at all times.

- While talking, eating or doing any other work, it helps to be aware of our actions to avoid doing anything inappropriate.

Aspects of Mindfulness to be Taken Care of by the Teacher

- Be an active participant in the process. For example, while getting the students to practise mindfulness, do it yourself too.

- Be aware of your mental state when you enter the class, and keep your thoughts and feelings stable. Remember, children notice the teacher's behaviour.

- Before you get the students to reflect, ensure the class is peaceful and that each student is comfortable. Ensure that the children share their experiences afterwards. Children would need a pleasant and safe environment to share their experiences.

- The whole idea of this exercise is not to get away from or suppress our thoughts and feelings. This exercise aims to make the children aware of their environment, emotions, thoughts and feelings so that they can respond better to their usual behaviour.

The Happiness Curriculum of Delhi Government Schools suggests very simple yet effective mindfulness methods for learners of all grades. All the teachers, irrespective of their context, or classroom setting, can help their students practice mindfulness as per their age group, using the simple types and techniques suggested by the curriculum.

The daily practice of Mindfulness focuses on paying attention, on purpose, in the present moment, and without judgement. Mindfulness practice involves focusing on one aspect of your experience at a time. Simply internalise the feeling and practice it anywhere and anytime.

There are many positive responses about the Mindfulness practice, which is the initial segment of the Happiness period daily. Not only students but also teachers benefit from this practice. Many students have vouched for the positive effects they have seen in themselves. For many students, it has been a transformative experience, from being underconfident to confident, timid to bold, and submissive to expressive. They feel better positioned to express themselves and think that the present is empowering and the only tool for change.

On observing and talking to students, they readily shared their individual journeys. Out of the many inspirational ones, a few of them have been mentioned here:

"I used to spend a lot of time playing video games on my phone, but as I started practising mindfulness more, I realised that I am not utilising my time properly. Gradually, I tried to reduce my screen time, and I started to involve my mother in mindfulness too."

— Rakshit Bharadwaj, Grade 7, Sec-9 Rohini (Name changed in order to conceal the identity of the student)

"I couldn't ride a bicycle without support until recently, but I decided to keep trying and not give up, and I finally managed to learn to ride my bicycle without support. I learnt that being in the present and focusing on my task at hand is all that makes a difference. I practise mindfulness in school as well as with my family at home." Shared Sparsh Agarwal gleefully, Grade 7, Delhi government school. (Name changed in order to conceal the identity of the student)

The core pedagogical principle behind the Happiness Curriculum in Delhi is that emotional intelligence and self-awareness can be triggered through self-expression and reflection.

All the mindfulness activities suggested for students are equally effective with teachers. They can help teachers to cope with their personal and professional challenges. Teacher's own social and emotional well being matters the most, thus they must raise their awareness level about their stressors and ways to handle them most effectively.

THREE TENETS OF DAILY MINDFULNESS

Mindfulness practised on a daily basis in the schools of Delhi Government has three fundamental tenets:

Step 1	**Mindfulness Check-in** STEPS OF THE ACTIVITY	3-5 Minutes

- Teachers should tell students that through this activity, we will take our attention off the work we were doing before this and bring our mind to the present. This exercise can be done by the students anywhere and at any time.

- Tell the students to sit comfortably, straighten their back and close their eyes. If someone finds it difficult to close their eyes then they can lower their eyes and look downwards.

- Tell the students to keep their hands on the desk or on their lap.

- Tell the students that we will begin the class with the mindful check-in activity. We will do this for 3 minutes.

- Tell the students to focus first on the sounds they can hear around them and then take their attention to their own breathing.

- Tell the students that the outer sounds may reduce or increase, they may be heard at intervals or heard continuously.

Wait for 20 seconds

- Tell the students to become aware of these sounds, however they might sound. Ask them to listen to where they are coming from.

Wait for 30 seconds

- Tell the students that now they should focus on their breath. Focus on inhaling and exhaling.

- Ask the students not to change the rhythm of their breath. Just be aware and focus on them.

Wait for 10 seconds

- Ask the students to focus on when they are inhaling and when they are exhaling. Is there a difference between the breath they are taking in and the one they are giving out? Are these breaths cool or warm, fast or slow, light or deep?

- Tell the students to be aware of each breath.

Wait for 20 seconds

- Now ask the students to slowly focus on how they are sitting and whenever they wish to they may open their eyes.

Step 2	**Discussion on Mindfulness** PROPOSED POINTS OF DISCUSSION	10-15 Minutes

- Ask the students to think about the changes they experienced within themselves during the process for 2-3 minutes. Ask them to think about the experience and the practice of the previous week's activity. Ask them to think also about where and when they used this activity other than the happiness period.

- After this, teachers can discuss with the students about the learnings and benefits of mindfulness and how it has improved their lives in ways like –

  o Reduction of stress within

  o More focus in the classroom

  o Realising what is going on within them (happiness, sadness, anger etc.)

- Tell the students that they may write their thoughts in their notebook. After this, some of them can share their experiences.

- In this period, a discussion can be held on the particular experiences, challenges or questions that arose during the mindfulness activity.

Step 3	**Silent Check-out** STEPS OF THE ACTIVITY	1-2 Minutes

- The mindfulness class should be ended sitting quietly.

- During this, a reflection should be made by the students on the thoughts and feelings generated by today's activities.

- Do not give any other instructions to the students.

- Whether the students want to close their eyes and reflect, or would want to lower them – this should be left on them.

Irrespective of the content, grade, context or infrastructure teachers can start mindfulness practice with their students and experience the transformation in the classroom energy. Given ahead are some of the most cherished mindfulness variations that our students are enjoying on different days of a week. All the mindfulness activities suggested ahead will follow the three fundamental tenets as given above.

For each activity, specific instructions and points to be discussed are given for your reference.

MINDFULNESS ACTIVITIES FOR CLASSROOMS

MINDFUL LISTENING

Mindful Listening: The steps of the activity

▶ Teachers must tell students that today they are going to be quiet and listen to the sounds around them. This is called Mindful Listening.

▶ Tell the students that they may sit in a comfortable position, straighten their backs and close their eyes. If someone is finding it difficult to close their eyes then they can lower their eyes and look downwards.

▶ Ask the students to focus on the various sounds that are coming from the environment. These sounds can be of the fan, the traffic outside, of someone talking or laughing.

▶ Ask the students to concentrate on the sounds they can hear in their environment. Ask them to just listen to them carefully without deciding whether they are good or bad.

▶ If anyone feels that their attention has drifted, they may become aware about it and focus on the sounds once again.

▶ After 1-2 minutes, ask the students to open their eyes and ask the class what all sounds they could hear. After this, take the activity ahead in the following manner:

▶ Tell the students that once again we will focus on the sounds, as it is possible that our attention might not have gone on some sounds earlier.

▶ Teachers must ask the students to sit in a comfortable position again, straighten their backs and slowly close their eyes.

▶ Teachers should ask the students to listen to the various sounds around them.

▶ They should pay attention to the kind of sounds that are there. Which among these sounds are coming constantly?

▶ The teachers should ask them to just listen to them carefully without deciding whether they are good or bad.

▶ If anyone feels that their attention has drifted, they may become aware about it and bring their focus back on the sounds once again.

Discussion on Mindful Listening

■ How did you feel during the activity?

■ Was there a difference in your experience between the first and second time?

■ Who all got distracted with the sounds? (You may ask them to raise hands.)

■ If you got distracted, were you able to focus again on the sounds?

■ What have we gained out of this exercise (Indication: Whenever we sit quietly and focus on different kinds of sounds, we tend to hear more sounds than what we would hear ordinarily).

MINDFULNESS ACTIVITIES FOR CLASSROOMS

MINDFUL BELLY BREATHING

Mindful Belly Breathing: The steps of the activity

▶ Tell the students that in Mindful Breathing, we bring our attention on to our breathing and focus on each breath that we inhale and exhale.

▶ Tell the students to sit in a comfortable position and close their eyes. If someone is finding it difficult to close their eyes then they can lower their eyes and look downwards.

▶ Now ask the students to pay attention to each breath that they inhale and exhale.

▶ Now ask them to keep one hand on their stomach.

▶ Ask the students to pay attention to when their stomach expands and when it contracts as they inhale and exhale along with focusing on their breath.

▶ Meanwhile, if it is seen that the students are not able to concentrate on their stomachs and breathing then the teacher should tell them that the stomach expands while inhaling and contracts while exhaling.

▶ After conducting the activity for 1-2 minutes, ask the group of students these questions:

:: Did you feel the stomach expanding?

:: Did you feel the stomach contracting?

:: When did your stomach contract?

:: When did your stomach expand?

▶ Now, conduct the activity once again for 1-2 minutes and once again ask the students to examine carefully the pattern of inhaling and exhaling and the stomach movement.

Discussion on Mindful Belly Breathing

■ Earlier, while breathing, did you pay attention to the stomach movement?

■ Why does the stomach expand on inhaling and why does it contract while exhaling?

■ Discuss that when we focus on breathing along with stomach movement our breathing becomes slower and deeper. We can do this exercise anytime and at any place.

■ By breathing deeply and mindfully how do we feel?

MINDFULNESS ACTIVITIES FOR CLASSROOMS

MINDFUL SEEING

Mindful Seeing: The steps of the activity

▶ Tell the students that today we will focus our attention on things around us.

▶ Ask the students what all they are able to see in class (Like chair, table, blackboard, duster, books, pen, window, fan, door etc.)

▶ Teachers should take the students' attention to any one thing like duster, fan, table, chair etc. Get their attention on the shape, form, colour, its positioning in the room etc.

▶ For example, while drawing the attention of the students towards their desks, the following questions may be asked –

:: Are you able to see the four legs of the desk?

:: Are all the four desks around you similar?

:: Is your desk broken from somewhere or has a scratch or mark?

:: Is the entire desk of one colour only?

:: How is this desk?

:: Hard or soft?

:: Rough or smooth?

:: Are you able to focus on any other property of this desk?

▶ In a similar manner, the attention of the students can also be taken to their books. Taking one book, you can ask them about various aspects of the book, like, Is this book:

:: Heavy or light? Small or big?

:: How many pages are there in this book?

:: What are the colours on its cover?

:: What is written on its cover? It is written in which colour?

:: Ask them to open a page in the book and ask –

:: This page is of which colour?

:: Are its letters big or small?

:: Is the writing on it shiny?

:: Is it embossed?

:: Is the page rough or smooth?

:: Are all pages like this?

▶ On the basis of the above stated examples, teachers can discuss any one point.

▶ Now ask the students to focus on any one thing that is attracting them.

▶ Ask the students to observe its shape, colour, positioning in the room, figure, material and its various parts carefully.

Discussion on Mindful Seeing

- Which objects did you focus on and what all did you see?

- Have you observed any object carefully like this earlier?

- How did you benefit from observing?

- **Where do you think paying attention is useful?** (Clue: When we look carefully, we are able to know whatever is happening in our surroundings in a better manner.)

BREATH STAR

Breath Star: The steps of the activity

▶ Tell the students that they may sit in a comfortable position.

▶ Ask the students to spread five fingers of one hand. This way, the hand will look like a star. This is the student's star hand.

▶ Ask the students to use the index finger of the other hand to draw the outline of the star hand.

▶ Now the students should take a deep breath and while inhaling they should take the index finger of the second hand through the bottom to top of the thumb of the star hand.

▶ Now, while exhaling, the students should be asked to bring the index finger of the other hand from the top of the thumb of the star hand to the space between the thumb and the index finger.

▶ Now, ask the students to inhale deeply and make the outline of the index finger of the star hand in a similar manner.

▶ Now, ask the students to exhale and while exhaling they should make the outline from the top of the index finger to the base of the second finger.

▶ Ask the students to repeat this pattern and trace the fingers of the star hand for five slow, deep breaths.

▶ Now, ask them to repeat this process with the other hand too.

Discussion on Breath Star

■ During the activity, did you focus on the breaths you inhaled and exhaled?

■ What was the difference between breathing like this and breathing normally?

■ What are the advantages of breathing mindfully and deeply?

MINDFULNESS ACTIVITIES FOR CLASSROOMS

STRENGTHENING THOUGHTS

Seeing our Strengths: The steps of the activity

► The teachers should tell the students, "We are going to practise mindfulness through one more activity today."

► Ask the students to peacefully sit in a comfortable position and close their eyes slowly and focus on the sounds around them.

Wait for 30 seconds.

► Tell the students that with the next breath they inhale, they should focus on themselves and take out time to think what are their qualities or what are they good at, what are their strengths? For someone, it can be academics, someone else may be a good friend or someone's quality may be his/her peaceful disposition. It can be anything.

Wait for 2 minutes.

► Tell the students that if they have all recognised their strengths, they may now spend some time in thinking about them. We all have some or the other qualities, but we are not able to recognise them.

Wait for 1 minute.

► Ask the students to take their attention to their feelings and how they are feeling after recognising their strengths.

Wait for 30 seconds.

► Ask the students to breathe in and when they feel good, they may open their eyes.

Discussion on Seeing our Strengths

■ Were you able to recognise your strengths?

■ Did you find it difficult to recognise any of them?

■ Would anyone want to share their experience?

■ How did you feel during this activity?

MINDFULNESS ACTIVITIES FOR CLASSROOMS

STICKY THOUGHTS

Seeing our Strengths: The steps of the activity

▶ Teachers will tell the students that today we will do an activity using our imagination. Now all the students should close their eyes, take three deep breaths and sit in a comfortable position. Now ask the students to imagine a big elephant. Imagine that this elephant is huge, it has big ears, black eyes and is standing still. Imagine this elephant in great detail.

Teachers should wait for 30 seconds and let the students imagine.

▶ Tell the students to not think of the elephant now. Any thoughts related to the elephant should be taken out from their mind. Sit quietly for a while but don't think anything about the elephant.

Teachers should wait for 30 seconds and let the students think.

▶ Ask the students if any of them is still visualising the elephant, they may raise their hands.

Discussion on Sticky Thought

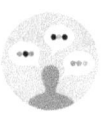

■ Were all of you able to imagine the elephant?

■ When I asked you not to imagine the elephant, what happened? (Clue: Most of the students would have imagined the elephant.)

■ When it was instructed to take off the elephant-related thought, still did some students imagine it? Ask the students to raise their hands. (Clue: Similarly, sometimes it is tough not to think about a topic. It means some thoughts, concerns and stressful thoughts get stuck in our minds. We can call them sticky thoughts as they don't leave our minds easily and keep recurring in our minds.)

■ If we try to calm our mind or will try to hinder these thoughts, does it become a tough process? Like, when I asked you not to think of the elephant you were still thinking of it.

■ If we are only aware about our thoughts but don't get caught in them, then how would we feel? (Clue: The mind becomes peaceful. Let your thoughts come and leave organically. Keep a sense of empathy with your thoughts and see that you don't get caught in them. Through this, slowly you will experience peace of mind.)

MINDFULNESS ACTIVITIES FOR CLASSROOMS

HAPPY EXPERIENCES

Happy Experiences: The steps of the activity

▶ The teacher should tell the students to sit in a comfortable position. Ask them to straighten their backs and loosen their shoulders. Slowly, let them close their eyes. Now, ask them to take a deep breath and exhale through their mouth. Repeat this once or twice. Take a deep breath and exhale through the mouth.

▶ Tell the students to think of a place or a situation where they feel happy and peaceful. Imagine what you'd do at this place or in this situation. Who are you with?

Wait for 10 seconds.

▶ Ask the students to search and find out where in their body they are experiencing happiness. Is it in their heart, their stomach or hands?

Wait for 10 seconds.

▶ Tell the students to experience this feeling of happiness. Students should pay attention to how they are feeling. What is the process going on in their body?

▶ Ask the students that with this they should also try to focus on their thoughts. This very second, what are the thoughts you are getting? Is it one thought or are they multiple? Students should be with these thoughts for a while.

Wait for 10 seconds.

▶ Tell the students to slowly breathe in ... and breathe out. While breathing in they should think, "I am smiling." While breathing out they should think, "I am smiling."

▶ Now ask the students to slowly focus on the environment around them and when they are ready, they can open their eyes.

▶ Now the students should look at each other and smile gently.

Discussion on Happy Experiences

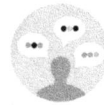

■ How are you feeling now?

■ When did you feel happy?

■ Did you feel happy imagining the place where you thought you'd be happy?

■ **What do you think are the advantages of practising this activity?** (Clue: Through continuous practice of this activity, we experience more positive feelings like happiness, love, contentment, gratitude, pride, hope, interest etc. Through this we feel more gratified and our well-being increases.)

MINDFULNESS ACTIVITIES FOR CLASSROOMS

THOUGHTS AS BUS PASSENGERS

Thoughts as Bus Passengers: The steps of the activity

▶ Teachers should start with: We have various kinds of travellers in a bus but the focus of the driver is on the road. Similarly, we are the driver of our attention and our thoughts are like bus passengers. In this activity, we will quietly observe the various kinds of passengers on the bus today.

▶ Teachers should tell the students: "Today we will observe our thoughts as if they are bus passengers. The way a driver does not focus on any passenger but concentrates on the road, in a similar manner, we will pay attention to our thoughts."

▶ Ask the students to see the thoughts the way they are. They should not think of them as right or wrong.

▶ Ask the students to sit in a comfortable position and loosen their shoulders. Take a deep breath and exhale through the mouth. With the next breath, close your eyes gently. If anyone is not comfortable with closing eyes, they may look downwards.

▶ Tell the students to become aware of their surroundings with the next breath. Tell them to take their attention to the sounds being created in their surroundings.

Wait for 30 seconds.

▶ Tell the students they are inhaling and exhaling normally. They should focus on the sensation caused by inhaling and exhaling.

Teachers should wait for 10 seconds.

▶ Tell the students to imagine that the thoughts coming to their minds are like the passengers on the bus. The way passengers get on and off a bus, similarly, thoughts are crossing your mind.

▶ Tell the students that they should not classify their thoughts as good or bad. If any thought passenger fights, gets angry or creates stress, they should take their attention off that passenger and bring their focus back to their own breathing without fighting with that passenger.

▶ Tell the students that while observing thoughts, they might get caught in them or get distracted. In such a case, they should bring their focus back to their breathing.

▶ Now, tell the students to observe their thoughts for the next one minute. Let the thoughts come and go. Do not stop them.

▶ Tell the students to bring their attention to their sitting position with the next breath and become aware of the sounds in their surroundings. Whenever they feel good, they can slowly open their eyes.

Discussion on Thoughts as Bus Passengers

■ How was your experience?

■ Would you want to share your experience?

■ When were you able to focus on your thought during the exercise?

■ How did you feel about paying attention to your thoughts?

MINDFULNESS ACTIVITIES FOR CLASSROOMS

GRATITUDE

Gratitude: The steps of the activity

▶ Teachers should tell the students that through this activity, we will focus on any one person, who is very important to us, and would express gratitude towards that person.

▶ Tell the students to sit in a comfortable position. Ask them to straighten their backs and close their eyes. If anyone has a problem in closing their eyes, they can look downward.

▶ Tell the students, for a few seconds, become aware of the person towards whom they are thankful and for whom they want to experience gratitude. They should bring their attention to the moments spent with that person.

Wait for 10 seconds.

▶ Ask the students to focus on where they are with that person.

Wait for 5 seconds.

▶ Ask the students to focus on what they are doing with that person.

Wait for 5 seconds.

▶ Ask the students to become aware towards that moment. Ask them to remember it and feel it.

▶ Tell the students to pay attention if the person is trying to say something to them. Ask them about how they feel about their relationship with that person? They should take their attention towards the kind of feelings they are experiencing at this moment and if they feel they are getting caught in the feelings, they can bring their attention to their breathing.

Wait for 10 seconds.

▶ Tell the students that with their next breath, they can express gratitude towards that person.

Wait for 30 seconds.

▶ Now ask the students that when they are expressing their gratitude towards that particular person, what is the kind of sensation in their body? Try to know with your next breath in what part of the body are you feeling that sensation. Is it in your throat, your chest, your hands, your feet, your legs etc. For a while, be with this sensation. With each breath you take, this feeling goes on increasing.

▶ Tell the students to gradually bring their attention towards their sitting position and whenever they feel ready, they may open their eyes.

Discussion on Gratitude

■ How are you feeling after this activity?

■ Whom were you grateful towards and why?

■ What will happen when you express gratitude towards others?

■ What can be the various ways in which you can express gratitude?

MINDFULNESS ACTIVITIES FOR CLASSROOMS

THOUGHTS AS TRAFFIC

Thoughts as Traffic: The steps of the activity

▶ Teachers should tell the students to sit comfortably and loosen their shoulders. Now, take a deep breath and release it from the mouth. Close the eyes with the next breath. If anyone is uncomfortable with closing the eyes, they may look downward.

▶ With the next breath, students should become aware of their surroundings. Take your attention towards various sounds in your surroundings.

Teachers should wait for 30 seconds

▶ Ask the students if they are inhaling and exhaling normally. Now ask them to imagine that they are standing by the side of a main road peacefully. They are watching the traffic on the road.

▶ Tell the students to imagine that the thoughts coming to their minds are like the vehicles on the road. Each thought is like a vehicle on the road. The way vehicles are coming and going on the road, similarly, thoughts are crossing your mind.

▶ Tell the students that they should not classify their thoughts as good or bad. They should not try to change or stop them. They should observe thoughts like traffic. Thoughts are coming, they are going and they are observing them with a quiet mind.

▶ Tell the students that while observing thoughts, they might get caught in them or get distracted. In such a case, they should bring their focus back to their breathing.

▶ Now, tell the students to observe their thoughts for the next one minute. Let the thoughts come and go. Do not stop them.

Wait for 1 minute.

▶ Tell the students to bring their attention to their sitting position with the next breath and become aware of the sounds in their surroundings. Whenever they feel good, they can slowly open their eyes.

Discussion on Thoughts as Traffic

■ How was your experience?

■ Did your attention go to your thoughts?

■ What did you feel about your thoughts? Did you feel a difference in your thoughts in the beginning, middle and end of the exercise?

■ Did you experience that some thoughts stayed longer in your mind as compared to some others?

MINDFULNESS ACTIVITIES FOR CLASSROOMS

MIND JAR

Mind Jar: The steps of the activity

Necessary objects: A transparent bottle and a fistful of chalk powder or mud. Teachers should demonstrate this experiment to the students:

▶ Show the students a bottle half filled with water. Ask the students if they can see through it. Is the water in the bottle stable and clean?

▶ Tell the students that this is the situation of our mind when we are peaceful and stable.

▶ Now fill a fistful of mud or chalk powder in the bottle or ask the students to do so and close the lid tightly.

▶ Now shake the bottle. Ask the students to observe carefully as the mud or chalk powder mixes with the water. Now ask them again how are they finding the water look? (Students can now see the water is unclean. It has become dirty and muddy)

▶ Tell the students that we get upset, angry, worried and uncomfortable in a similar manner. At that time, we are unable to think clearly and aren't able to decide on what is right or wrong.

▶ Now keep the bottle on the table and ask the students to take their attention on their breath and take five deep breaths.

▶ Now ask them to observe the bottle for a while.

▶ Tell the students to pay attention to how they are feeling now?

▶ Ask the students to pay attention to where the mud/chalk powder is going in the bottle.

▶ When most of the mud/chalk powder particles settle at the bottom and the water starts appearing clean then you can finish the activity and move towards the discussion.

Discussion on Mind Jar

■ What happened after mud/chalk powder was put in the water?

■ In which situations does our mind feel uncomfortable and worried?

■ After leaving the mud/chalk powder in the water for a while, how did the water appear at the end?

■ How can we stabilise our mind?

■ Don't you feel when our mind is calm like this water, we feel nicer? Why/why not?

■ When we are under stress, we often get carried away by our feelings and do something wrong. If, in that situation, we bring our attention to our breathing, we would be able to decide better with a calm mind.

MINDFULNESS ACTIVITIES FOR CLASSROOMS

PROGRESSIVE MUSCLE RELAXATION

Note: Refrain the students from straining too much during this exercise, they should only do the steps to the extent comfortable to them. If anyone feels uneasy during this exercise, they should discontinue doing it.

Progressive Muscle Relaxation: The steps of the activity

▶ The teachers should tell the students in a simple language that Progressive Muscle Relaxation is an activity through which we take our attention towards the tension and relaxation being generated in our muscles.

▶ Ask the students to imagine that they are holding a lemon. Now they should imagine that they are squeezing the lemon to take out its juice. While doing this, they will experience a stress in their muscles. They should feel this tension. Now students should imagine that they have dropped the lemon. They would be able to feel the tension in their muscles has reduced.

▶ Ask the students how they are feeling.

▶ Now, ask the students to peacefully sit at one place and close their eyes. Tell them to focus their attention only on their body. If they get distracted, they should take their attention back to the same muscle on which they were focusing earlier.

▶ Now, the students should make a tight fist with their right hand. Ask them to hold this fist for five seconds and feel the tension rising in their hands. Now ask them to open the fist gradually and loosen their hand. Let their hands rest. Students should repeat this activity once more.

▶ Now, ask the students to make a tight fist with their left hand. Ask them to hold this fist for five seconds and feel the tension rising in their hands. Now ask them to open the fist gradually and loosen their hand. Let their hands rest. Students should repeat this activity once more.

▶ Now ask the students to make a tight fist with both hands but without putting stress. Now they should experience the tension rising in both their hands. Now open the fists and loosen the hands.

▶ Ask the students to loosen their entire body.

▶ Now ask the students to tighten and straighten their hands and arms. They should straighten them as much as possible. Now, feel the tension rising in the arms. Wait for 5 seconds. Now let the hands relax and loosen them. Feel the relaxation in the hands and arms.

▶ Students should feel the relaxation in their whole body and breathe normally.

Wait for 10 seconds.

▶ Now tell the students to raise their eyebrows as much as they can and tighten their forehead muscles. Wait for five seconds and feel the increasing stress on the forehead. Now relax and loosen the forehead muscles. Relax completely.

▶ Tell the students to feel the increasing relaxation in their bodies.

▶ After this, ask the students to close their eyelids and tighten their eye muscles. Wait for five seconds and then loosen the eyelids. Loosen them completely. Feel the increasing relaxation on the eyelids.

Wait for 10 seconds.

▶ Now, tell the students to put their necks backwards as if they are looking at the wall. Feel the tension in the neck muscles. Wait for five seconds. Now, gradually bring the neck back in place. Loosen the entire body and now feel the increasing sense of relaxation in the whole body.

▶ Continue to breathe normally.

▶ Now ask the students to rotate their shoulders as much as possible. Feel the tension in the shoulder muscles. Now, gradually relax the shoulders.

▶ Ask the students to feel the state of relaxation in their neck and shoulders.

Wait for 10 seconds.

▶ Now ask the students to take a deep breath and gradually release it.

▶ Breathe in ... and gradually breathe out.

▶ Ask the students to focus on how they would be feeling peaceful, relaxed and stress-free. Now feel the relaxation in the entire body.

▶ Ask the students to mentally count from 1 to 4 and then back from 4 to 1. As and when they feel ready, they may open their eyes.

Discussion on Progressive Muscle Relaxation

■ How are all of you feeling?

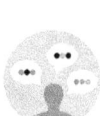

■ When did you experience stress in your body and when did you feel relaxed?

■ What is the difference between tightening your muscles and loosening them?

■ What are the advantages of this practice?
 (**Indication:** When we feel stressed our body and muscles also feel the stress. By practising Progressive Muscle Relaxation our body relaxes because of which our mind also feels peaceful.)

■ (Stressful thoughts » Stress in the body » Progressive Muscle Relaxation » Relaxation of the body » Relaxation in the mind)

TEACHER'S HAPPINESS

High accountability, repetitive content, and diversified tasks make teaching a challenging and stressful profession. Teachers who are able to take control over the stress are more likely to steer the classroom towards positivity and productivity irrespective of the challenges and difficulties around. When teachers resumed their classroom teaching after a long gap of covid-19 induced pandemic they had to face several academic and behavioural learning gaps in their students which were enough to increase the stress level of many teachers except those who knew how to handle the stress and find the seeds of opportunity and optimism in any given stressful situation. These were the teachers who knew the art of being happy and creating a happy classroom.

The OECD (Organisation for economic co-operation and development is an intergovernmental organization) in 2020 presented teachers' stressors in the TALIS 2018 results. The TALIS (Teaching And Learning International Survey) 2018 is a large-scale survey of teachers, conducted in 48 countries. According to this survey, There was not a big difference between teacher stress levels across contextual and educational levels. The stress levels for teachers were similar from elementary to high school. Some of the major stressors found during the study were,

- Having Extra Duties due to absent teachers
- Having too many lessons to teach
- Having too much lesson preparation
- Addressing parents/guardians concerns
- Maintaining classroom discipline
- Keeping up with changing requirements from authorities
- Having too much Grading/Marking
- Being Held Responsible for students' achievements.
- Having too much administrative work

Other than these top universal stressors for teachers, a teacher might also feel stressed in pursuit of

- Striking a work-life balance
- Lack of autonomy
- Scarcity of resources
- Non-recognition of efforts

- Prejudices and nepotism.

To deal with these stressors, teachers need a coping mechanism. A mechanism that can help them deal with professional pressures and personal challenges. Some of the key ideas that have been proved to be successful for bringing change in the perception of stress from Distress to Eustress.

- Mindfulness

- Periodic Focussed Group Discussions

- Meditative exercises

  ○ Drawing Mandala/Any art form

- Physical Exercise

  ○ Muscle Relaxation

- Professional Learning Networks (Clubs or groups with similar interests).

- Peer Learnings and Celebrations

- Planning and Execution of tasks according to the priority.

- Barrier free communication with learners, colleagues, and seniors.

- Participation in cultural activities.

- Conferences, Seminars and webinars on social-emotional well beings.

- Pursuing hobbies and interests.

Teachers who have gained control over their thoughts, emotions, actions, choices and health are more likely to steer their classroom through thick and thin. Teachers who are happy look out for opportunities to engage with their learners and other stakeholders. They have learnt the art and the science of classroom happiness. It enables and empowers them to create happiness within and around.

2

ENGAGEMENT
BEYOND ENJOYMENT AND ENTERTAINMENT

Engagement requires that students know they've been heard, that their voice matters.

— Douglas Willms

We, humans, as social beings, often like to live, learn and laugh in a group together. If observed keenly, we reach our optimum potential when we find ourselves socially acceptable by our tribe. Isolation or segregation is something that works like slow and lethal poison.

Likewise, our classroom students love engaging in different activities with their peers. The fun of learning together, falling down, and then picking up the courage to lift your spirits again by having deep-rooted trust is the beauty of collaborating for a unified cause.

Simon Sinek has also said, "A team is not a group of people who work together, but a group of people who trust each other."

Let's discuss a small anecdote where one of the dynamic teachers created magic in the classroom with her little students. It was one of the student-led Saturday Special days. The highly enthusiastic teacher explained the concept of the J.A.M. (Just a Minute) activity to the class. It was very clear from the beginning that the students would have fun and feel a sense of responsibility that day. Large groups and small groups, along with individual presentations, were planned by the teacher.

In this activity, students were made aware of the rules of the action. All 47 students of the class were divided into groups of 5, each through a process of a random selection of teams. One child was assigned to track the scores of the team and keep a watch on the allotted time, and another was designated to conduct the session. The teacher decided to be the "Guide by the Side" and not the "Sage on the Stage." The students responded to hold the class with different roles and were explained the significance and gravity of the part allotted to them. Following that, the rest of the groups of students were told that a bowl with different topics written on different chits would be offered to them. In the two-minute window period, they would brainstorm on their chosen topics.

After that, a group representative who was previously selected by the team would be asked to come forward in front of the class and present the opinions of his group in front of all the students. The timekeeper ensured that the activity goes for every group strictly for Just a Minute, as the name suggests. A different kind of positive collaborative energy filled up the entire class. All the students were involved in some aspect of the program. The bright ones supported the not-very-bright ones in overcoming their fear of being judged or the fear of being wrong. Instead of following teacher-directed instruction, students develop interdisciplinary skills and critical thinking to keep them intellectually engaged in learning. The autonomy and the onus of taking the class proceedings ahead charged up the atmosphere with the jubilation of collaboration, engagement, and bliss.

The Glossary of Education Reform defines student engagement as "the degree of attention, curiosity, interest, optimism, and passion that students show when they are learning or being taught, which extends to the level of motivation they have to learn and progress in their education."

In his book "*Creative Schools*," Ken Robinson makes a vivid distinction between learning and education. He writes, "The fundamental purpose of education is to help students learn. Doing that is the role of the teacher. But modern education systems are cluttered with every sort of distraction. Political agendas, national priorities, union bargaining positions, building codes, job descriptions, parental ambitions, and peer pressures exist. The list goes on. But the heart of education is the relationship between the student and the teacher. Everything else depends on how productive and successful that relationship is. If that is not working, then the system is not working. If students are not learning, education is not happening, something else may be going on, but it's not education."

Learning is most effective when teaching is natural and connected—connected not just with the learners but also with the curriculum. Learner-centred education has teachers at its centre, centred entirely on children. Thus, the primary objective for teachers is to establish a deeper connection with their learners by engaging them in meaningful and contextual learning experiences.

ENGAGEMENT IN THE CLASSROOM

How can student engagement be improved in the classroom? Are there places where small changes would significantly impact your teaching practice?

Douglas Willms got to the heart of the matter when he noted: "Engagement requires that students know they've been heard, that their voice matters."

Use techniques that make students involved and active partners in the teaching-learning process. When students feel encouraged and supported, there's no limit to what they will accomplish. This is where the happiness of a teacher and student is evident.

As mindful teachers, let us be conscious of every student in our classroom. Think for a moment when you pose a question in class. Is it just a few students who are answering or all? We're sure that you would have answered it yourself. There are a lot of simple, doable, yet effective personalised learning techniques that can encourage every student to get involved in your lessons. Some of these strategies are elaborated below.

Classroom Agreements

To create connection and community in a classroom, it must be a psychologically safe place for students to share. Nothing is more damaging to an honest, open discussion than a hurtful comment. Great teachers collaborate early with students in the classroom and build consensus on how they want to treat each other.

The teachers talk to students and share that they want their class to be a powerful and positive experience for all learners. They create some rules on how they'll interact and treat each other. The teacher then asks the students to define those rules.

For those of you who have done this, you know that it is very impressive to hear the rules the class comes up with. They are very similar to the rules you would define; however, because the students define them, they help enforce the rules and hold one another accountable. They can then be called Classroom Agreements, as all the students discuss and agree to abide by those agreements mutually.

Students' Journals

Our success in transforming our classroom by letting students tell their stories started with providing students with the opportunity and guidance to capture their thoughts and feelings in personal journals.

By empowering our students through our own stories, we were able to create conversations to build a common basis of understanding, which became the foundation for transformation and connection.

Journaling has the guaranteed benefits of reducing anxiety, decreasing stress and depression and even mental disease. It helps us develop self-awareness and manage adversity and conflict in our lives. Moreover, this reflective time is one great time for student motivation. It increases their ability to stay committed to dreams and goals of their life. This engagement with their dreams helps them reach towards the realisation of their dreams.

Students as Leaders

Most of us feel vulnerable while speaking in public, particularly in front of peers. Presentation exercises are a great facilitator of connection and support within a classroom, as well as a golden opportunity for students to support one another truly.

There is also no better way to meaningfully engage students than to take them from the passive listening mode and bring them into the active mode of presenting or participating in their small group discussions. The more we get our students presenting and sharing, the more connections and a greater sense of community will be built.

One such innovative initiative started in government schools of Delhi is "Project Voices." This Project started with a vision to enable all students to enhance their confidence regarding oratory skills in both languages, namely English and Hindi. The core intent of the project is to give voices to the unheard and faces to the unseen. Instead of organising competitions, it aspires to involve all students and make it a regular classroom activity. A plethora of activities, namely- Spell Bee, Extempore, Debate etc., has made our students come out of their shells and face their stage fears. It has made them confident and more expressive and able to present their thoughts and beliefs more coherently and cohesively. A programme based on similar aspirations for the development of spoken skills of students is running in the state of Punjab, India, by the name of *"English Booster Club"*.

Icebreakers

Well-thought-out and appropriately timed icebreakers (simple, short, interactive activities) are other excellent tools for connecting students in classrooms. Such activities get students moving and interacting with each other. They add an element of fun and engage the students in joyful ways. And, just as with public speaking and presentations, icebreakers make them a bit vulnerable. Brené Brown has put it perfectly, "When we are vulnerable, we are beautiful."

Icebreakers create energy and allow students to look at the better and more positive aspects of the rest of the students in the classroom. This new perspective lays the foundation for a connection that's so critical to engaging them. In one of the online workshops with

In-Service teachers, a teacher asked participants to use the chat box to mention their name, meaning, and the story behind naming them. This activity not only familiarised the facilitator with the names of the participants but also developed their instant interest in each other and created a high level of engagement for the rest of the session.

Field Trips/ Nature Walk

In one of the wonderful books titled The Last Child in the Woods by Richard Louv, he chronicles a staggering separation between children and the outdoors, then connects this with many of the alarming and rapidly rising trends in our children, such as obesity, anxiety and depression.

It is essential for us to be on the outside. It makes us feel small (in a good way) and puts things in perspective. For students, it might just be a breath of fresh air and removes students from the very environment that causes stress and anxiety in their lives. It takes them away from technology and the wires that are binding and disconnecting our generation X. It brings fresh and renewed energy to your classroom, new opportunities to have meaningful conversations and builds relationships between you and your students or among students themselves.

During our N.E.T. (National Exposure Trips) to various schools in India, we got the opportunity to visit some of the exemplary schools where practices like Nature Walk, Environment Drives by students, and Awareness Campaigns etc. are an integral part of their school curriculum. For example, Prakriya Green Wisdom School (Bangalore) has kept one period daily for students of kindergarten to 8th to go out of their classroom and take a walk around the huge garden in the school. Students go with their pens and pads to note their observations. It helps them to contextualise and concretise their learnings.

Similarly, students from schools like Muni International (Delhi), Rishi Valley (Andhra Pradesh), T.V.S. Academy (Tamil Nadu) and Star Academy (Tripura) take pride in their close connection with nature.

Likewise, whenever students are taken out for school excursions or field trips sponsored by the school for meritorious students, it sets a perfectly fresh and fertile ground for the seeds of "Being a part of one school family" to be nurtured

Perform a Class Service Project

Class service projects is an opportunity for students to come together. There is something powerful about helping another human being and knowing you have the ability within yourself to make a noticeable difference. The most powerful part of the Service Project is the debrief, wherein the students talk about their personal experiences. These discussions really allow them to shine and bring out their best in front of their peers.

Mobilising your class around a team-based project of any kind can be really powerful, but doing something that exposes them to others who need them the most, is the most transformative experience of all. It's a fantastic way to foster connections and relationships in the classroom.

Charles Shultz once said, "In life, it is not where you go; it is who you travel with." We believe when all is said and done, and we look back, it will be the relationships we had and the connections we made that will mean the most to us. Nothing is more energising than a positive and meaningful exchange with another human being. Suppose we can foster an environment of community and trust in our classrooms. In that case, we can find that vibrant energy and infuse it into students so they can fulfil their potential and maximise their positive impact on the world.

Quick Breaks

Bring quick breaks into your classroom to get students up and about! These are quick exercises or activities that allow students to channelize some extra and stored energy. In the middle of your class, pause for some moments to do something that refreshes the students and gets them rolling with the classroom activities.

There's no limit to what you can do during a quick break, but here are a few of our favourite ideas:

- Sing a quick song

- Play a round of silent ball

- Bring an inflatable beach ball to bounce around the room, but don't let it touch the ground.

- Start a freeze dance party -- play some music and bust a move, but challenge students to freeze in place when you pause the tunes.

Out of these different ideas, find one or two that work for your students.

Popsicle Stick Names

Write every student's name on a popsicle stick and put it in a mug. When you need learners to answer from the class, pick up a popsicle stick and ask the student whose name appears to share their response.

Wait Time

Recall when you last posed a question in class. Do you give them a few seconds or maybe a minute to think over the question that has been simply flung at them. Is this performance pressure not enough for them that your command, "Hurry Up! Do you know the answer or not," adds to the existing woes. Giving students the much-needed space to answer will help them develop confidence.

They will be able to gain access to their previously known information successfully.

Whip Around

Pose a question, then walk around the room and ask every student to contribute by sharing his views. If they have the same answer as another student in the class, that's not an issue! Encourage them to rephrase it differently to boost the confidence of the entire class.

GAMIFICATION
Energy-Excitement-Engagement

Irrespective of age and experience, games infuse energy and excitement into the class. By introducing game-like elements into our classrooms or workshops, we can enhance the level of engagement and help our participants learn better. Gamification is different from Game-Based Learning. While the latter is about playing games in the classroom, the former is all about bringing the elements of games into the process of learning.

Gamification is the preparation of a mindset where students are not afraid to try, fail, and try a level again until they succeed. They willingly take turns and share ideas to come up with solutions. Effective teachers bring the magic of games into the everyday experience of the learners.

It helps them to make their learners:

- **Take Ownership:** Allowing students to make meaningful choices along with understanding the reason of their choices gives them more control.

- **Rise Up from Failures:** Emphasising "Play again" rather than "Game over" creates a more relaxed and positive atmosphere for students to experiment with new approaches and ideas.

- **Track the progress:** Progress indicators are significant to show students where they started, where they're heading towards and how close they are to their goal.

- **Stay motivated:** Though rewards are an extrinsic motivator, but they can still be very effective in developing skills and knowledge. And who knows – they may lead to intrinsic motivation for learning!

- **Collaborate:** Both games and learning can be social activities. Gamification provides an opportunity to be in a team or be in competition with classmates to achieve new levels of mastery.

- **Keep going:** The more engaging the learning, the more students will want to dive in and swim further.

- **Gamification is Easy and Fun:** To include gamification in our teaching, we need not modify our entire lesson plan or revamp our content. Indeed, it is a fairly easy activity to be integrated along with the existing learning activities.

Ideas for Gamifying Learning for The Learners

Badges

Award badges to students as and when they meet certain defined thresholds for different tasks, assignments, standards or even class participation. Each category provides different "levels" of challenge and achievement. It helps make that sense of accomplishment accessible to everyone in the class. It also allows students to display their badges for others to see and encourages camaraderie – or competition.

Level-up

On introducing a "level-up" system with experience points that can be traded in for rewards at certain intervals. Students can watch their progress bars fill up as they complete their work or achieve class objectives. Once they reach certain levels, they can use them as individual rewards (like getting extra computer time) or combine them together for class rewards (like having a five-minute dance party). It's essential to give students a choice regarding how they'd like to gather points, so make sure to include a wide range of activities when planning how they can be earned.

Leaderboards

Create a sense of competition with leaderboards. Leaderboards display the total points each student has earned, giving the high-scorers a sense of accomplishment and motivating their peers to improve their game in search of that top spot. Beware, leaderboards can be really demotivating to students at the bottom, so use them with sensitivity and care.

Quests

Turn assignments into quests. Role-playing games often follow a narrative and give the player choices that may have different outcomes. In a classroom example, students can choose between fiction and non-fiction reading, which then branches off into different genres and sub-genres, inviting students to "choose their own adventure". This is purely based on what interests them most.

Skill Up

Map your curriculum with skills. Just like in video games, we can unlock new levels as we skill up through practice and persistence. So it can be emulated for the classroom's learning objectives, where students need to master certain standards or skills before they can unlock the next one.

Steps to Gamify

Like any effective classroom strategy, gamification isn't just about enjoyment and entertainment. A solid, gamified lesson plan starts with a few well-thought-out steps:

Analyse The Need For Gamification

Gamification is all about meaningful engagement and immediate motivation. Thus a teacher shall gamify the classroom areas where these elements are most required. A critical analysis of the learners' needs and the lesson's demands will help teachers identify such areas and plan to gamify accordingly.

Know What They Know

Integrate your lesson plan with game mechanics your students already know. If they're into subway surfer or temple run, put more emphasis on collecting achievements and rewards; if they're more into the battle genre like Pub-G or Clash Of Clans, class competitions may provide that extra force to be the "last kid standing."

Establish The Rules

All games have rules. Discuss with the class how your gamified approach works, and outline their routes towards advancement… and rewards in the form of badges, gifts, or titles.

Make It Flexible

Students should choose how they want to progress based on their abilities and interests. For example, there should be multiple ways to earn points.

Map The Curriculum

Think big. Look for different opportunities to add gamification that connects with subjects and with learning from previous years. You can even work with other teachers to create cross-class goals that turn learning into an adventure that lasts for times to come!

Track your own progress

Is your gamified approach working? You will know only when you measure your own

SCORE CARD TEMPLATE FOR GAMIFICATION IN CLASSROOM

(Mark the weekly classroom gamification indicators for each individual on the scale of 0-5. Add up the score to select and award the winners with titles like star performer, Ms/Mr. Punctual, etc.)
** 0 stands for least and 5 stands for the maximum

Attendance	
Behaviour	
Act of Kindness	
Academic Performance	
Active Participation	
Leadership Roles	

progress toward your classroom goals. It is a fun opportunity to set up a scoreboard for yourself.

Always remember, your main focus is to make your curriculum and lessons more engaging throughout, not just for fun but to help advance student learning.

In simplest terms, gamification in the classroom correlates with increased student motivation and engagement.

Score card or Leader board template for Gamification

There are ample ways to associate daily or regular activities with the point system, but it need not be complicated. So to make students interested in the gamification of education, we recommend using a points system so that students earn rewards for their weekly performance. A sample scorecard or leaderboard template is given below for your reference.

- Attendance here means regularity in school.
- Good behaviour can encompass words like empathy, humane, and sensitivity towards all, to name a few.
- Exceptional kindness, like helping an absent student with the notes for the previous day.
- Academic achievement is where the child can secure good grades in his classroom academic assessments.

Every student enjoys recognition and reward for what they're doing. Can you imagine how charged up the classroom would be when gamification aids learning? In addition to boosting student engagement, gamification can also improve classroom behaviour, rewards and content delivery and processing.

Another significant concept that goes beyond engagement is collaboration. Collaborating is more than just cooperation and coordinating. It calls for aligning energies, sharing resources, and working in perfect harmony towards a common purpose. The next segment of the chapter explores the rationale and resources for collaborative learning and collaboration of teachers through clubs and conferences.

COLLABORATIVE LEARNING

"Coming together is a beginning; keeping together is progress; working together is a success."

~Henry Ford

Educational experiences that are active, social, engaging, contextual and student-owned lead to deeper learning. Collaborative learning is an effective approach to developing higher-level thinking, oral communication, self-management, and leadership skills. It creates opportunities for interactions, exposure, and understanding of diverse perspectives. It also promotes active listening and critical thinking. Despite knowing the many benefits of collaborative learning, teachers find it difficult to implement collaboration in large-sized classes with varied aptitudes, skills and learning levels of students.

Ideas to Inculcate Collaborative Spirit in our Learners

- Introduce group or peer work in the semester to set clear and discreet student expectations. Once they taste the sweetness of peer work, there will be no looking back.

- Establish Community Agreements for participation and contributions. Ideally, these statements should be positive, short, and a maximum of 5 in number. These agreements are democratically created and then curated by those students in the class who will abide by them.

- Plan for each stage of group work. A meticulously planned work is always something that yields better results. It is often said, "Sweat more in training so that you bleed less

If...

A. **You want to ensure that each student is engaged in the discussion.**
   Pairs

B. **You have some very vocal students who intimidate others.**
   Pairs or triads, putting the vocal students together

C. **Your students are at various levels in their understanding. You want the ones who are struggling to be able to listen a lot.**
   Mixed-ability groups

D. **Your students are at various levels in their understanding. You want all students to be able to contribute at their own level of understanding.**
   Same-ability groups

E. **You want to encourage good turn-taking and conversational ability.**
   Triads doing pair work with one functioning as listener or recorder

F. **You want to give students a chance to think about an issue or answer on their own first before sharing it.**
   Think–pair–share (Thinking alone, then sharing with a partner, then sharing with a small group)

in war". Plan and prepare well to be in a better position to execute well.

- Abraham Lincoln said,' "If I only had an hour to chop down a tree, I would spend the first 45 minutes sharpening my axe." Carefully and clearly explain to your students how groups or peer discussions will operate. Based on it, students will be graded thereafter. Your timely guidance will give more clarity to the task to be executed by the students.

- Consider using written contracts. Deal with your learners in black and white as a concrete reminder instils a greater sense of responsibility rather than having some vague information stored in the mind that sometimes starts to fade away also.

- Incorporate self-assessment and peer assessment for group members to evaluate their as well as others' contributions. When a culture of learning from peers is awakened, the classroom pedagogies run on an autopilot mode.

Examples of Collaborative Learning or Group Work Activities

Stump Your Partner

- Students take a minute to create a challenging question based on the content taught that day.

- Students pose the question to their partner.

- To take this activity a step further, ask students to write down their questions and hand them over to you. These questions can be used to create tests or exams. They can also be reviewed to gauge student understanding and guide the teacher further in planning her lesson.

Think-Pair-Share

- The instructor poses a question that demands analysis, evaluation, or synthesis.

- Students take some time to think through an appropriate response.

- Students turn to a partner (or small groups) and share their responses. Take this a step further by asking students to find someone who arrived at an answer different from their own and convince their partner to change their mind.

- Student responses are shared within larger teams or the entire class during a follow-up discussion.

Catch-Up

- Stop at a transition point in your lecture.

- Ask students to turn to a partner or work in small groups to compare notes and ask clarifying questions.
- After a few minutes, open the floor to a few questions.
- Once questions are answered you may continue with the lecture.

Fishbowl Debate

- Ask students to sit in groups of three.
- Assign them their roles. For example, the person on the left takes one position on a topic for debate, and the person on the right takes the opposite position. The person sitting in the middle takes notes and decides which side is the most convincing and provides a reason for his/her choice.
- Debrief by calling out a few groups to summarise their discussions.

Case Study

- Create four to five case studies of similar difficulty levels.
- Make students work in groups of four or five to work through and analyse their case study.
- Provide 10-15 minutes (or adequate time) to work through the given cases.
- Walk around and address questions if any.
- Call on groups randomly and ask that students share their analysis. Continue until each case study has been addressed.

Team-Based Learning

- Start a course unit by giving students some tasks, such as reading or project assignments. Consider assigning these to be completed before class.
- Check students' comprehension of the material with a quick multiple-choice quiz. Have students submit their answers.
- Assign students to groups and have them review their answers with group members to reach a consensus.
- Keep a record of both the individual student assessment scores and the final group assessment score (both of which are used toward each student's course grade).
- Deliver a lecture that specially targets any misconceptions or gaps in knowledge

the assessments reveal.

- Give groups a challenging assignment, such as solving a problem or applying a theory to a real-world situation.

Group Problem-Solving

Many instructional strategies involve students working together to solve problems, including inquiry-based, authentic, and discovery learning. While each has unique characteristics, they fundamentally involve:

- Presenting students with a problem.
- Providing some structure or guidance toward solving the problem. However, they are all student-centred activities in which the instructor may have minimal roles.
- Reaching an outcome or solution.

Self-learning and a reflective atmosphere created by collaboration help achieve multiple targets directly or indirectly, and the happiness of achievement is beyond expectation when it comes to the teacher's expectation. An effective teaching-learning approach always advocates effective group and pair work in a classroom which are the fundamental routes to productive collaborative learning. It allows students to talk about their learning, ask questions, and apply concepts to new situations.

However, these types of activities must be thoughtfully engineered and appropriately used to be effective. (TESOL,2009). Choosing Group Size and Composition is not an easy task and has various constraints attached to it. Depending upon the level and needs of students as well as the content to be delivered, students are paired for various tasks.

Below is a list of the most efficient pair and group works according to different situations. The list works as a compass or a radar to set the direction of the classroom towards positivity and productivity.

Tips for Effective Implementation of Group and Pair Work

Group and pair work ignite brainstorming and thought processes in the learners. It becomes pertinent for teachers to implement these activities effectively and consistently. Below are some simple tenets for implementing collaborative learning in its true spirit.

- Introduce the activity.
- Be sure to state the goal.
- Model what students will need to do.

- Provide any vocabulary or information that students will need.
- Give detailed instructions, possibly in writing. Check for clarification by having students restate the instructions or model the activity.
- Divide into pairs or groups and begin the activity.
- Monitor the activity by walking around the room.
- Stay available but not intrusive.

ENGAGING LEARNERS IN CLASSROOM ACTIVITIES AND MANAGEMENT

The teaching-learning process in a classroom or any social gathering works best if the members are given respect and autonomy to choose. In a classroom, it can be seen in the active participation of the learners in managing the classroom processes and choosing matters, methods, and modes of learning.

Teachers who have successfully engaged their learners mostly have successfully involved students in managing classroom routines and making individual and collective decisions.

American English State Government (*www.americanenglish.state.gov*) suggests several classroom jobs for young learners that can be used according to the needs of any classroom. We have used some of the following successful interventions with our primary-level students. We have been suggesting all of these to our trainees to improve their classroom culture and student participation leading to greater autonomy for learners.

Assigning Roles As Per The Context And Competencies

- **Line Leader:** The first student in line is in charge of stopping at designated places along the route and maintaining appropriate speed.
- **Door Holder:** Holds the doors for students in line all along the travel route to the next class or for the next period.
- **Last in Line:** The last person in line closes or locks doors after Door Holder completes the job.
- **Monitors:** Watches out for classmates and, if need be, redirects students in the bathrooms, at the water fountain, during recess, etc.
- **Lighting Director:** Turns lights off/on when entering or leaving a room or as requested.
- **Librarian:** Keeps the classroom library organised and assists with the issue and

submission of books as needed.

- **Board Cleaner:** Cleans the board as needed/requested.

- **Paper Passer:** Passes out papers/assignments.

- **Paper Collector:** Collects completed papers/assignments.

- **Supply Manager:** Hands out and collects necessary supplies.

- **Attendance Taker:** Checks to see which students are absent.

- **Computer/Media Helper:** Turns computers/technology off/on daily or as needed.

- **Errand Runner:** Delivers items or messages to different parts of the school as needed.

- **Homework Checker/Collector:** Checks that students have completed homework and/or collects it as requested.

- **Cleanliness Monitor:** Checks around the classroom to ensure that students have cleaned up after activities, the floor is clean, and desks are tidy.

- **Plant Waterer/Animal Caretaker:** Waters plants and feeds classroom pets.

- **New Student Ambassador:** Helps any student who is new to the classroom to learn rules, schedules, expectations, etc.

- **Emergency Assistant:** In charge of carrying the class emergency bag (which has the attendance list, first aid kit, and any other emergency items) on all outings and drills.

- **Substitute(s):** Completes the job of any student who is absent that day.

Suggestions For Assigning Tasks

In order to give students a chance to perform tasks that they will enjoy, teachers can spend time explaining all of the roles at the beginning of their session. Then, ask all students to list at least five tasks they are interested in doing. They can also assign multiple students to work together in the same role.

For larger classes, it is almost impossible that every student may be able to hold a job all the time. Try to split up the time and roles so that all students have a chance to do a classroom task at some point in the year. Tasks can be changed often, but students should have enough time to learn about their responsibilities and become comfortable in their roles.

Many teachers change student jobs according to the length of a grading period or term (quarter, trimester, semester, etc.). Each time you change tasks, refer to the students' lists and basically try to assign each learner a task from their interests.

Giving Autonomy to Learners

As teachers, we try to assign our students tasks, homework, and projects to complete by expecting them to follow instructions and submit their work. However, giving options to learners helps them take responsibility for their performance and feel responsible and invested in their work.

When given autonomy, students often choose assignments that they find interesting and that they feel are important.

Choices can promote motivated learning, accountability and positive attitudes.

Assignment Ideas for Learners to Demonstrate Understanding and Learning

- Make a poster that talks about what you have learned. Then share it through a presentation or gallery walk.
- Write a paragraph/essay to compare and contrast two concepts or describe an event from the story/book.
- Complete a graphic organiser with important information about the topic.
- Write and perform a role play, or create a video with a small group of classmates.
- Work with your elbow partner to write a script for an interview with an important character from the story. Conduct the interview in front of the class.
- Create an art project (drawing, collage, model, etc.) that illustrates what you have learned and present it to the class or display it in a gallery walk.
- Create a quiz about the most important things you think someone should know or remember after learning about this topic. Make an answer key for the quiz.
- Match descriptions with words or pictures, or categorise characteristics or details as per the topics or ideas you have learned about.

When it comes to giving options to learners, teachers can make a small start. Students do not have to have a list of choices for all of their work. Begin by thinking of a few options for assignments at the end of a unit.

For instance, as a summative project after reading a book, give students the choice of making and presenting a poster about a character, conducting an interview with a character, or writing a journal entry from a character's perspective. It would also help to create examples of the work to give students information about what the assignments include.

As you become comfortable offering different options for these types of tasks, you may also think of different ways to incorporate choice into daily assignments. Grading different types of assignments often seems confusing. But relating the tasks with the curriculum standards and objectives will make it quite clear what you expect students to be able to do in order to demonstrate mastery of the content.

Learners feel they are an important part of the classroom community when they have a chance to share ideas and make suitable and selected choices. By involving learners in rule-making and daily classroom management tasks, teachers build trust and positive relationships with students. Learners develop a sense of personal responsibility and independence through classroom tasks and assignment choices.

By incorporating these ideas in the classroom, teachers can promote engagement and positively impact young learners' academic and social development.

An autonomous classroom results from deep trust and mutual respect between teachers and learners. It provides a fertile ground for sowing the seeds of independent thinking, creativity and leadership. Bringing autonomy to the classroom not only helps learners to feel valued and accomplished but also supports teachers in discovering the hidden and latent talents in their learners. The environment of an autonomous classroom is usually lively and energetic; here, learners explore their own and their peers' nature, skills, and interests.

In February 2020, just before the first Covid pandemic in India, we went to Kerala for an educational tour. As a part of this N.E.T. (National Exposure Trip), we were taken to a small school in a remote village. The school was an excellent example of finding learners' autonomy in real and in action. Starting from the general school discipline to everyday classroom activities, teachers were there to guide and support only if needed; otherwise, it appeared to be a student-powered school.

We were amazed to see the successful running model of F.L.I.P. teaching (discussed in detail in Chapter 5). The student's discipline committee, active participation of students in making the annual calendar of school activities, interaction and involvement of students with community representatives, preparation and presentation of issues and concerns with administration. Last but not least was the active role played in designing and conducting lesson plan activities with the help of their teachers that included transaction of the content and its assessment.

Students in this school were happier and more confident; they were more contributory and took ownership of their own learnings and classroom experiences. Learners' autonomy is not just about giving freedom to choose but to contribute, collaborate, and coordinate with peer for governance and teaching learning experiences.

Teachers with the dexterity to pass on the baton to their learners are more likely to bring real happiness in the classroom with authentic and substantial growth in their learners' abilities and life skills.

3

AWARENESS
KNOWING IS THE BEGINNING

"Meeting the needs of all students starts with knowing who your students are. "

— Elena Aguilar

etting to Know You (GTKY) is quite a popular term among trainers, teachers and coaches who envisage introductory activities where participants get to know about each other. It is a general observation through our specific experiences with workshops, teacher training, and classroom teaching that when participants know a bit about their fellow participants, they feel a sense of familiarity and belongingness. It creates a psychologically safe environment, thus creating conducive conditions for the seeds of happiness and positivity to grow into a happy classroom.

The OSD (Officer on Special Duty), School Branch at DoE (Directorate of Education), Delhi, B.P. Pandey, shares that for anyone, especially for leaders of an organisation, it is an added advantage if one can share a very special connection with your team. This connection could be established by simple acts such as remembering the full names of your team members, their personal and professional trouble areas that they had discussed with you at some point of time, their strengths and weaknesses and providing them with an environment of autonomy. Once you genuinely ask about their well-being and preferences, you instantly click with them, and it gives you an edge to strengthen the bond of trust and concern between you and your team.

TESOL (Teaching English to Speakers of Other Languages) is one of the renowned international organisations for English language teaching. It conducts international conferences, creates teaching-learning materials, spreads awareness about innovations and interventions in classroom teaching of English, publishes books and courses and has many branches worldwide. One of the most appreciated books by TESOL press is "The

6 Principles for Exemplary Teaching of English Learners" by Deborah.J. Short, which recommends six core universal principles for any effective English language classroom.

The first of these 06 principles is "Know Your Learner", which states, "Exemplary teachers learn basic information about their students' families, languages, cultures, and educational backgrounds to engage them in class and prepare and deliver lessons more effectively."

Why to know about your Learner?

Teachers can best adapt instructions to students they know well. Learn about your students' cultures and experiences. Use that background information as a resource for classroom learning, stock classroom libraries, and plan projects.

Getting to know you is the first and foundational step of any progressive classroom. Teachers who know their learners well develop a better connection with their learners. Teachers may start by gathering basic information like the students' cultural and language backgrounds, demography, interest areas, talents, special needs, family members, life goals, etc.

Over a period of time, we have realised the significance of the words "Education" and "Learning" the former is derived from the Latin word, "Educo", which means "To draw out", and the latter is a process of "Acquiring knowledge, practising skills, and developing attitude". So, suppose we see teaching and learning as a process of education. In that case, we may define it as "A continuous process to draw out information, abilities, and values from the learners to help them grow."

Teachers may use daily informal conversations to draw out information about the learner, or they may use a more formal way to collect the data and use it effectively to create a connected, thus happy classroom.

"Happy teachers go an extra mile to learn about their learners and make sure to let them know they are known."

Connected Classrooms are Happy Classrooms

Creating a holistic and all-inclusive classroom is another significant step toward creating a positive classroom culture where learners will have respect, tolerance and a feeling of oneness among themselves.

Classrooms where teachers and learners are connected, respect individuality, work in collaboration and embrace challenges together are the classrooms where positivity breeds and happiness prevails.

Knowing about the learners is the beginning, and if done correctly, it becomes a strong foundation for a happy and productive classroom. The information collected about the learners will be of no use if the teacher fails to leverage that information and make effective use of the information to build connections, design content, and adapt lesson plans while delivering.

What to know about your Learner?

"Knowing breeds familiarity, and familiarity breeds connect."
Teachers begin to know about their learners, and the more they understand that the teacher knows them, the more interested and invested they become in school. Teachers can have innumerable avenues and aspects to learn about their learners.

Each and every aspect of a learner's life plays an important role in shaping the overall future and identity of the learner. Thus, teachers who want to breed happiness in their classrooms always seek information about their learners. They use every possible way to gather knowledge about their learners' such as

Native Language

Many children lack interest in education because they're missing some degree of personal connection with the things they're learning. These children connect emotionally with their learning when instructed and involved in their native language. This connection can harness itself to a greater appreciation for one's education and

Mr. B.P. Pandey, Directorate of Education, GNCT Delhi

"All mentors are my family and I feel for them as closely as I feel for my family members. The bond of mutual trust that I share with my team of more than 250 mentors is really unique. They feel quite confident to speak to me about any problem that they are facing. At the same time they are always willing to go even overboard when I ask them for any particular task. I am really proud of my trustworthy team."

culture and foster a positive relationship between the taught and the education system. Language also helps foster a sense of belongingness. Many children may be struggling to fit into their schools or communities. They may sometimes feel as though they need to abandon their existing roots, and their cultural differences set them apart from other kids. Still, teaching them how important it is that we foster diversity and how valuable culture is to enrich our experiences is much required.

Family and Friends

Knowing a slice of their life or coming to terms with their close ties, that is, family and friends enable the teacher to make informed choices while interacting with them and designing classroom learning experiences related to sharing their real-life interactions.

Access to Books, Technology, etc.

Knowing the learners' interests and expertise in the kind of books they like to read or have read or how well-versed they are with technology gives first-hand information to the teacher. With this, she may be able to introduce concepts like Peer learning or buddy system, community support, classroom libraries etc.

Specific Choices

Being aware of the preferences and choices of our learners is of great value to the teacher. It helps them design their classroom environment and curate the lesson plans accordingly. For example, children's favourite cartoon shows, preferred indoor and outdoor games or their favourite superheroes can be integrated with the lesson to make the process more involving and interesting.

Academic performance & Challenges

It would help the educator empathise with the learners and provide the necessary scaffolding to strengthen their learning abilities and successfully overcome their academic challenges.

Preferred curricular & Co-Curricular Activities

School and classrooms are the field areas where these aspects of the child's personality are discovered and honed. Thus, a teacher must provide multiple opportunities and platforms to highlight their children's inherent and hidden potentials through activities like debate, extempore, painting, etc.

Habits & Hobbies

Hobbies allow children to tap into their inner passions and talents while allowing them to understand all that they enjoy and are good at. This helps them build confidence and self-esteem, apart from giving their mind and body the much-needed stimulation. This information about the students can help the teacher provide the much-required push to the students to help them realise their interests and potential to the fullest.

Critical Medical Needs or Child's Medical History

It would help the teacher gain control over situations that need immediate attention and medical care in case of a medical emergency with the student at school. Every teacher mothers the children in the school premises, and she is in charge of the situation in case the child meets with an injury or if there is a relapse of his/her medical condition.

Learning Preferences

Teachers who know their students well and understand their uniqueness help them navigate the often under confident, confusing and anxiety-filled lives they lead. Teachers need to know their learners' preferred learning styles. This knowledge will help them plan their classroom lessons to match or adapt their teaching and provide the most appropriate and meaningful activities to suit every learner group at different stages. Stacking a teacher's portfolio with knowledge of learning styles and Gardner's Multiple Intelligence Theory will help you reach out to all your students, not just a selected few. Remember that all learners have unique strengths and weaknesses, and a one-size-fits-all approach to teaching doesn't cater to a student's individual needs.

VARK Model

The VARK model of learning styles emphasise four main categories of learners: Visual, Auditory, Reading/Writing, and Kinesthetic. The model suggests that students learn best when the teaching methods & school activities match their learning styles, strengths, and preferences. (Infographic given on the next page)

Activities to know about your Learner

Once we know what needs to be known and have clarity about the purpose and rationale behind knowing our learners, then ways and means to know are not difficult but rather a fun and engaging process. The process is to engage ourselves and our learners in knowing each other. All the suggested activities for knowing the learners are easy to do, involve low or no cost and require the least resources.

What's in a Name?

It is an introductory activity where learners/participants are given 3-5 minutes to think and gather information about their names, like the meaning of the name, does it have

VARK
Learning Style

The VARK model of learning styles suggests that there are four main types of learners: visual, auditory, reading/writing, and kinesthetic. The idea is that students learn best when teaching methods and school activities match their learning styles, strengths, and preferences.

Visual Learner	Auditory Learner	Reading Learner	Kinesthetic Learner

Visual learners understand new information best when they can **see** it, whatever it is.	Auditory learners understand best when they can **hear** it rather then see it.	If you take hand writing notes, the act of **typing** them can help your review.	They understand new information best when the **feel or do it**, when they can experience the learning
Colors, Graphs, Charts, Diagrams, Maps & Plans	Discussion, chat, guest speaker, recording, stories.	List notes, text formats, Book Reading.	Senses, Practical exercises, role-playing, Hand-on activities

a different meaning in some other language, and what is the story behind their name. Who gave you this name? Do you like your name, why or why not? How do you spell, write and pronounce it in your home language? Learners are then asked to share, What could they find in their name?

Teachers may write the prompts on the blackboard, use a projector screen, or may simply speak that for the learners. Learners feel valued and involved when they share their own stories and perceptions with the class in their own language with ease and confidence.

Pictorial Autobiography

It is a project-based activity where students are given 5-7 days to collect information about themselves and supporting evidence like photographs or articles. Learners are guided to arrange the pictures in chronological order of events and to weave an autobiographical story around them. These pictures not only include photographs from the present and the past but also of their future aspirations and dreams.

This activity holds immense potential to explore and discover a lot of significant facts and perceptions about the learner. It creates opportunities for practising presentation skills and developing an attitude of mutual acceptance and appreciation.

Board Games

Board games have always been a great idea to engage learners in small groups for interesting conversations. Some of the board games are explicitly designed to draw out information from the learners, like some of the language board games, which have been quite popular for getting to know each other, are given in the book, Activate Games for Learning American English, by the US state government is a collection of games for the language classroom. The board games offer interactive English language practice in a learner-centred, low-stress environment but some of them have been used effectively by us to know our learners as well as to engage our learners to know about each other.

ACTIVITY:
Board Games

Have you Ever...
Oh! When?

This activity gives practice regarding common conversations by asking and talking about past experiences. For example: Have you ever felt scared before speaking on the stage? Oh! When?

How to play?

- Have players sit in groups of 3–4.

- Determine who goes first and continue the game clockwise or counter-clockwise.

- Each player rolls the dice in turn.

- On their turns, the players move their game pieces along the path in accordance with the number indicated by the dice.

- In the space where they land, the players read the question aloud.

- The players respond to the question. If the answer is 'Yes,' players have to mention the last time they did the activity. If the answer is 'No,' players should tell something that they have done that is related to the prompt they have just read.

- The game continues until one or all players reach the 'Finish' space.

HAVE YOU EVER...
Oh, When?

Start...We're so ready!

Have you ever swam in a river?

Have you ever watched a baseball game?

Have you ever traveled by train?

Have you ever traveled to another country?

Have you ever cooked dinner for someone?

Have you ever kissed an animal?

Have you ever been to another continent?

Have you ever worn a hat?

Have you ever sung a song in a car?

Have you ever missed an English lesson?

Have you ever read a novel in English?

Have you ever slept outside, under the stars?

Have you ever eaten spicy food?

Bad luck! Go back 10 spaces.

Have you ever eaten sushi?

Have you ever borrowed money from a friend?

Have you ever played a piano?

Have you ever seen a ghost?

Have you ever climbed a mountain?

Have you ever lost your cell phone?

Great Job, Finish!

Source: "*Activate*", a book published by the US English Language Department for the use by teachers and trainers of English as a Second Language.

ACTIVITY:
Board Games

Name Your Favourite

This activity provides an opportunity for students to talk about their favourite things in a variety of categories. For example- My favourite hero, My favourite holiday destination etc. "Name Your Favourite" gives students practice using vocabulary and expressions they may need to talk about themselves in English.

How to play?

- Have players sit in groups of 3–4.

- Determine who goes first and continue the game clockwise or counter-clockwise.

- Each player rolls the dice in turn.

- On their turns, the players move their game pieces along the path in accordance with the number indicated by the dice.

- In the space where they land, the players read the question aloud.

- The players respond to the question. If the answer is 'Yes,' players have to mention the last time they did the activity. If the answer is 'No,' players should tell something that they have done that is related to the prompt they have just read.

- The game continues until one or all players reach the 'Finish' space.

NAME YOUR FAVOURITE

Source: "*Activate*", a book published by the US English Language Department for the use by teachers and trainers of English as a Second Language.

ACTIVITY:
Board Games

About Me

This activity allows students to express their opinions and preferences about several different topics/perspectives that they individually have.

How to play?

- Have students (the players) sit in groups of 3–4.

- Determine who goes first for the game and whether the turns will progress in the clockwise or counter-clockwise direction.

- Each player rolls the dice in turn.

- On their turns, the players move their game pieces along the path according to the number indicated by the dice.

- Players then finish the sentence written on the space (called a "prompt" or a "cue") where they land, using personal experience, critical thinking and/or skills imagination.

- Note that some spaces in About Me, penalise players and require them to go back to an earlier space. These are meant to increase the "chance" aspect of the game and foster mildly negative feelings for a moment, but it is all in the good spirit!

- The game continues until one or all players reach the 'Finish' space.

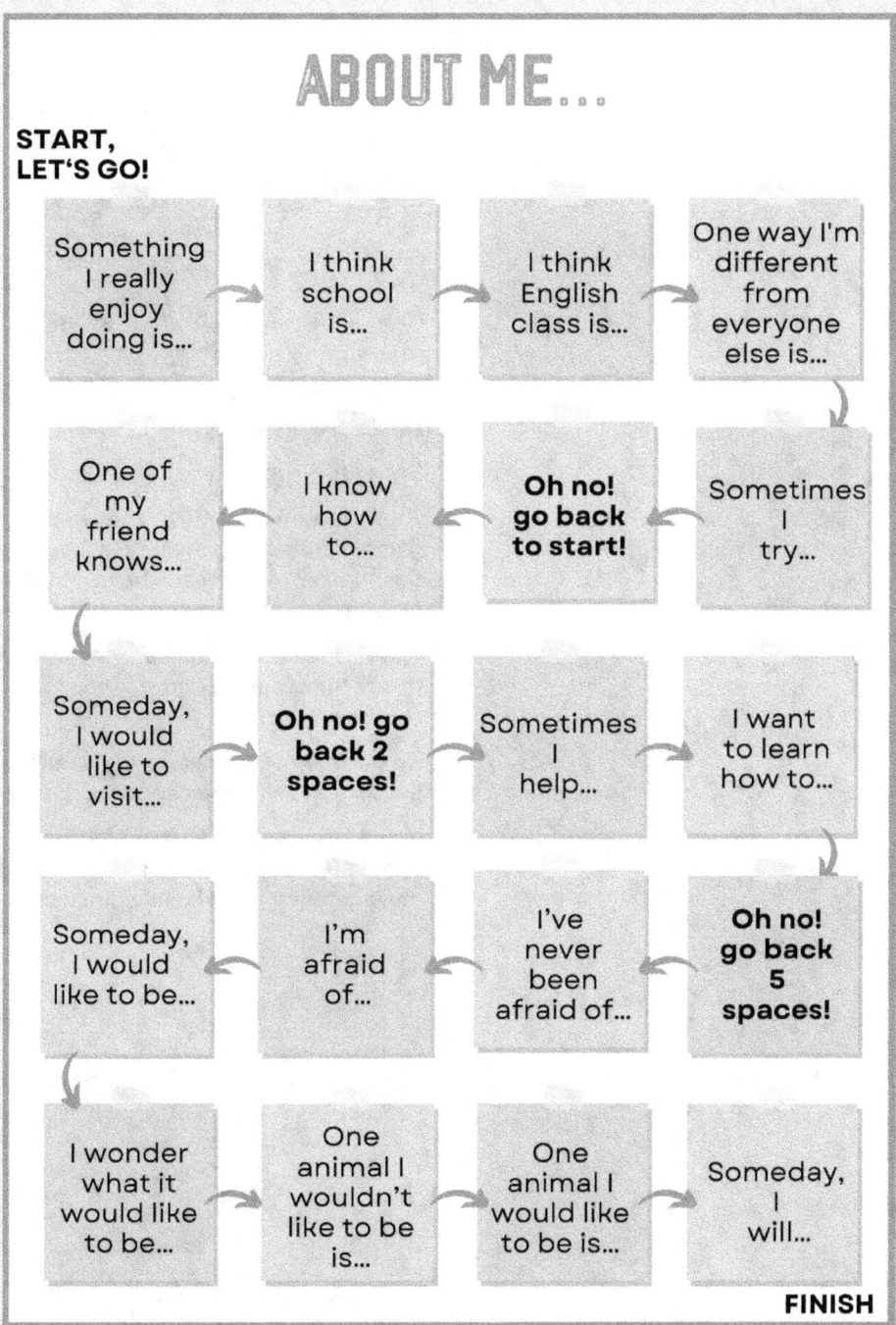

Source: "*Activate*", a book published by the US English Language Department for the use by teachers and trainers of English as a Second Language.

ACTIVITY:
Board Games

Name 3

This activity provides students with an opportunity to think critically and creatively and stretch their vocabulary to express their ideas about each topic.

How to play?

- **Have students (the players) sit in groups of 3–4.**

- **Determine who goes first and progress clockwise or counter-clockwise.**

- **Each player rolls the dice in turn.**

- **On their turns, the players move their game pieces along the path according to the number of spaces indicated by the dice.**

- **When players land on a space, they have to say three things according to the received topic.**

- **No player is supposed to say something that has already been said by anyone else.**

- **The game continues until one or all players reach the 'Finish' point.**

NAME 3

Start: we're off

Places You'd like to go someday. Why?	Language you would like to speak. Why?	The best things about your country.
The worst things about your country at the moment.	Talent or skills you'd like to have (but don't). Why?	Places You would like to visit in your country
OH NO! Go back to start!	Things you've learnt in the past week.	Things you have never done.
Important events in your life. Why?	Things you've bought in the last week.	**OH NO! Go back to start!**
Foods you never get tired of.	Jobs it would be interesting to have.why?	Things you like to do on weekends.

FINISH: Now name any 3 things your fellow players have said.

Source: "*Activate*", a book published by the US English Language Department for the use by teachers and trainers of English as a Second Language.

ACTIVITY:
Board Games

Would you Rather...Why?

This activity gives students an opportunity to express their preferences on a number of different topics. For example, would you prefer a holiday in the hills or near the sea?

How to play?

- Have players sit in groups of 3–4.

- Determine who goes first for the game and whether the turns will progress in the clockwise or counter-clockwise direction.

- Each player rolls the dice in turn.

- On their turns, the players move their game pieces along the path according to the number indicated by the dice.

- In the space where they land, the players read the choices aloud.

- The players select one of the possibilities and then say what they would rather do or be (even if the idea may be imaginary and really impossible). The players should explain their choices.

- The game continues until one or all players reach the 'Finish' point.

All the board games listed above and many more are part of "Activate", a book published by the US English Language Department for the use by teachers and trainers of English as a Second Language. It can be accessed by scanning this QR code.

WOULD YOU RATHER. WHY?

START, LET'S GO!

be a baker, a dentist, or a musician?

visit Ireland, Japan, or Hawai?

Learn Arabic, Spanish, or Chinese?

Live in a house or an apartment?

have perfect job or perfect partner?

drink coffee, tea, or juice right now?

Bad luck! go back 4 spaces

ride on an elephant, a camel, or a whale?

be a turtle, a dolphin, or an eagle?

visit the past or the future?

eat pizza, pasta, or ice cream every night?

Be 1.5 meters tall or 2.5 meters tall?

Work as a cook, a lawyer, or a librarian?

Bad luck! Go back to start.

Bride in a helicopter, submarine, or rocket?

have a bird, a monkey, or a cat as a pet

know how to play the guitar, violin, or drums?

be able to fly or have the power to be invisible?

be really wise or really lucky?

write a book, act in a film, or make a lot of money?

FINISH...

Source: "*Activate*", a book published by the US English Language Department for the use by teachers and trainers of English as a Second Language.

S.W.O.C. Analysis

Teachers may explore such activities or ideas to draw out more information from their learners. One such activity that has been used worldwide by adults for self-analysis is SWOC or SWOT analysis.

We conducted this self-probing activity with our learners of grade 6th, and above and the results were phenomenal. Before doing it with your children, it is strongly recommended that you do it for yourself. It will not only help you to understand the tool better but will also give you an opportunity to know yourself better.

With the help of parents, the learner himself and the peer group, teachers may prepare a SWOC chart to enlist an individual's strengths, weaknesses, opportunities and challenges. The learner then keeps this chart, and a copy of it is marked with the teacher.

Teachers may then help the learner to magnify the strengths and opportunities and prepare to deal with weaknesses and challenges.

During a candid intearction with our coordinator and mentor Mr. B.P. Pandey, OSD, School Branch at Directorate of Education (DoE) about the importance and ways to know about our learners, he heartily shares, "I am close to my people so I ensure to provide a psychologically safe space for my learners or team members. It makes them feel confident to share their professional as well as personal challenges or achievements. It makes me feel alive and connected when my team members open up with me. They freely talk about their realisations with self or coordination with others or the spoil sports in their project teams. 'One on One sessions, FGD (Focussed Group Discussions) and 360 Degree Feedback' are some of the interventions that I found to be extremely useful for knowing about our team mates. On a regular basis, mentors are given time slots to have a candid and fear free hearty talk with me. They talk about all kinds of difficulties that they face. It might be related to the work environment in their mentee schools, their coordination with their Heads of Schools or even colleagues with a closed mindset. After giving a patient listening to their areas of concern, I try to shift

"One on one sessions, FGD (Focussed Group Discussions) and 360 Degree Feedback' are some of the interventions that I found to be extremely useful for knowing about our team mates."

– B.P. Pandey

S.W.O.C. ANALYSIS
for Teachers

S

Strengths
What do you do well? What resources do you have? What advantages do you have over your competition?

Weaknesses
Know what areas need improvement, what your teaching lacks, and what hampers you from success?

W

Opportunities
Identify what opportunities exist around you, is there career growth, and is the perception of your teaching positive?

O

Challenges
What are some of the challenges faced by you? Is there someone or something that might be a threat to you or your teaching?

C

their focus from the problem to the solution that can be sought. This really eases them. But then again I need to personally know about their strengths and weaknesses from an external agency also. For this reason I have started taking their work and conduct report from different agencies like their Principals, colleagues, District Coordinators, Programme Managers to name a few. This approach for digging out the information about our team members and strengthening the connection can also be used by teachers in their classrooms to know more and better about their learners."

Adopting various approaches to dig out information about learners is a great idea to discover and strengthen bond with our learners. All the approaches and strategies to know about our learners or team members will open up channels of communication but the teacher needs to have effective communicative skills to reap the maximum from the opened channels.

Don Graves Activity

Don Graves, an educator who has helped reshape the teaching of literacy. It is a great litmus test that ascertains how well we know our students.

How it Works

- Make a three-columned chart on a piece of paper or a simple table/spreadsheet.

- In the left column, write down your students' names in the same order in which you remember them. (Who do you remember first? Who do you struggle to remember?)

- Now in the middle column, write down one positive thing that you have noticed about each student that doesn't have anything to do with schoolwork. (Joseph likes horses. Jai likes skateboards. Bani loves her grandmother.)

- In the third column, put a checkmark if you have talked to each student about this piece of knowledge. This helps us understand how well we know our students and also how well they know us!

- For students whom you struggled to remember or for ones you didn't know enough about, make a commitment to connecting with them in the next few days.

My Heritage-My Pride

It is a project-based activity to dig deeper into the learner's background, religious beliefs and moral values. It helps to create a culture of familiarity and association. Gay writes, "When we provide opportunities for students to discuss differences or conflicts among cultures and analyse the variations between the mainstream culture and other cultural systems, we enable students to learn about and honour other cultures and their ethnic identities. We help students develop positive cross-cultural relationships and teach them to avoid perpetuating prejudice, stereotyping, and racism. The goal is to create a learning environment in the classroom that encourages diverse learners to celebrate and affirm one another, work collaboratively for mutual success, and dispel powerlessness and oppression." (Gay, 2010)

How it Works

- Learners are divided into pairs or small groups based on common cultural or language backgrounds.

- Learners are given time and access to resources to gather information about the culture & heritage of their native places.

- Learners are encouraged to talk to their family and relatives to gain more details about their cultural and traditional roots.

- Learners take notes individually but work in small groups to collate the information and curate the presentation.

- The gathered information is then presented with the help of chart papers, bulletin boards, digital screens, or role plays.

- Peer reflections and questions after the presentation help reinforce students positively and provide valuable data for the teacher to design learning experiences.

Teachers who understand the significance of knowing about their learners are more likely to make stronger and deeper connections with them. Activities and games suggested above will help to create a culture of familiarity and belongingness.

EFFECTIVE COMMUNICATION: KEY TO CONNECT

> *"Effective Communication is the respectful exchange of thoughts, feelings, and belief between a speaker and a listener in such a way that the listener interprets the message in the same way as the speaker intends it."*
> – Central Board of Secondary Education, India, Teachers' Manual on Life Skills

Apart from using specific strategies to know about learners, a teacher may adopt a style of communication where learners may feel safe to confide in and confident to share. The skill of communicating ideas and the art of responding to learners help to earn the trust of the learners. Teachers who have mastered the art of responding face fewer difficulties in their everyday teaching as well as in life. They have a deep understanding of the significance of the response. They have understood the equation of events, responses, and results.

EVENT + RESPONSE = RESULT

Life is a continuous process of events happening all around us at all times. Events may occur without any prior notice or warning, or they are beyond our control, just like we can't predict an earthquake or a sudden fight among students in our classroom. Each event demands a response and, in turn, produces results. Thus, results depend primarily upon the responses.

Happy and progressive teachers are skilful communicators. They are responsive and not reactive. They understand the psychology of their learners and the onus of results on their responses. They understand the art and the science of effective communication.

There is the essential difference between those who can communicate effectively and those who can't. Studying communication and observing people communicating has led to the conclusion that communication is natural and inherent. Still, effective communication is a science and can be learnt through observation, experience and, above all, practice. To understand effective communication, we can take an analogy of computers which communicate efficiently and effectively to produce precise output on the basis of input.

Communication is a three-step process that begins with input, goes through a process, and finally comes out as an output. The swiftness and accuracy of these steps lead to effective communication. We have organs to receive the input, organs to process and organs for the output. When it comes to communicating in a particular language, the first and foremost step is to decide on the input, which depends purely on the desired or required output.

The initial step for anyone trying to improve their communication skills would be to realise and internalise that communication is not just a skill which can be learnt, practised, and improved—still, an attitude to be acquired and knowledge to apply.

Communication is effective if:

- Speech has clarity, and speed is optimum.

- The tone and pitch of the voice are according to the message being conveyed.

- Words are chosen carefully.

- The message is short and crisp.

- The message is clearly, completely, and confidently articulated by the sender.

- The message is clearly, completely, and contextually comprehended by the receiver.

- It is persuasive and inquisitive in nature.

- It is wrapped in positive and constructive enthusiasm and humour.

- It is natural and original.

- It is error-free and comprehensively fluent.

- It is empathetic and comforting.

Effective communication begins with the awareness of the three major elements of any communication. They can also be seen as the fundamental process of any communication. These elements are input, process, and output. Whatever messages we receive in the form of sounds and symbols are the inputs that are then processed in our minds and then spoken or written out as an output.

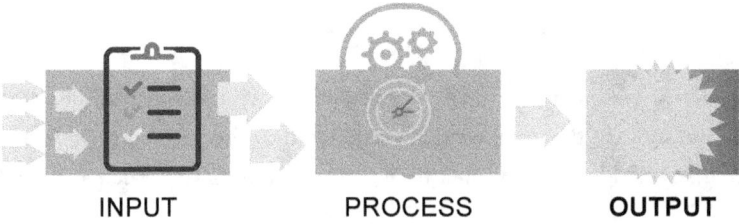

INPUT   PROCESS   OUTPUT

Here input can be compared to any event that takes place in and around our life; the output can be seen as the result based on the responses, which can be compared to processing.

Central Board of Secondary Education (CBSE), India, in one of its Teachers' manuals on Life Skills, recommends pointers for effective communication as mentioned below.

Non-Verbal Pointers:

- Maintain eye contact.

- Facial expressions such as smiling and nodding should be used to show interest.

- Body language and gestures should be confident and non-domineering.

- Optimum distance should be maintained so that you are near enough to be heard and far enough not to feel suffocated.

Verbal Pointers:

- Your words should match your body language.

- Ask both specific and open-ended questions to check if the other person understands.

- Avoid hijacking the conversation.

- Keep your tone clear and respectful.

- Let the other person finish sentences, do not interrupt.

- Summarising, paraphrasing, restating or asking specific questions shows your interest and understanding.

Communication between any two people is fundamentally an exchange of ideas and emotions, as mentioned in the definition above; thus, it becomes pertinent to encode the idea with vocabulary and sentence structures in accordance with the level of the receiver or the listener and the listener also decodes the message in its truest manner or as intended by the speaker or the sender.

The primary and most critical aspect of any verbal communication is listening; to make it effective, listening needs to be active.

Active Listening

In our daily lives, we engage in many conversations with friends; family members and co-workers. But most of the time, we don't listen to the other person as well as we should. We're often distracted by a lot of other things in the environment, such as the internet, the television, our cell phones, etc. We think we are listening to the other person, but in reality, we're really not giving them our full attention.

Active listening is all about building rapport, trust and understanding. By learning the skills below, one becomes a better listener and actually listens to what the other person is saying — not just what you want to hear or what you think they are saying. Active listening is a proven psychological technique that helps people express themselves verbally. It also makes a person more confident, comfortable and connected.

Active Listening Involves

- Being open to learning something new so that you can focus on what the other person has to say.

- Spending more time listening than talking.

- Guide the conversation using one or more of the Active Listening Skills.

- Summarise what the other person is saying from time to time to ensure you understand them correctly.

- Think about why the person is telling you this at this particular moment, and think about the meaning behind the words.

- Are you as good a listener as you think you are?

Steps To Improve Active Listening Skills

Below you will find different skills that help people be better active listeners. You do not have to become adept at each of these skills to be a good active listener. But the more you do, the better you'll be at. If you even use 3 or 4 of these skills, you will find yourself listening and hearing more of what the other person is saying to you.

- **Restating:** To show you are listening, often repeat what you think the person said, and that will not be by parroting the same lines but by rephrasing what you heard and then using your own words. For example, "Let's see if I'm clear about this. . ."

- **Summarising:** Bring together the facts & pieces of any problem to check the basic understanding. For example, "So it sounds to me as if . . ." or, "Is that it?"

- **Minimal Encouragers:** Use brief, positive prompts to keep the conversation going and show you are listening — for example, "umm-hmmm," "Oh?" "I understand," "Then?" "And?"

- **Reflecting:** Instead of just repeating what has been said, reflect the speaker's words in terms of feelings — for example, "This seems really important to you. . ."

- **Giving Feedback:** Let the person know what your initial thoughts are on the situation. Share pertinent information, observations, experiences and insights. Then listen carefully to confirm.

- **Emotion Labelling:** Putting feelings into words will often help a person see things more objectively. To help the person begin, use "door openers" — for example, "I'm sensing that you're feeling frustrated. . . worried. . . anxious. . ."

- **Probing:** Ask questions to draw out information from the person and get deeper and more meaningful information — for example, "What do you think would happen if you...?"

- **Validation:** Acknowledge every individual's problems, feelings and issues. Listen openly and with empathy, and respond interestingly — for example, "I appreciate your willingness to talk about such a difficult issue. . ."

- **Effective Pause:** Deliberately pause at key points to lay emphasis. This will tell the person you are saying something that is very important to them.

- **Silence:** Allow for comfortable silences; it will slow down the exchange. Give a person time to think as well as talk. Silence can also be very helpful in diffusing an unproductive interaction.

- **"I" Messages:** When you use "I" in your statements, do not focus on the person but on the problem. An I-message lets the person know what you feel and why — for example, "I know you have a lot to say, but I need to. . ."

- **Redirecting:** If someone is showing signs of being overly aggressive, angry or agitated, this is the time to shift the discussion to another topic.

- **Consequences:** Part of the feedback may involve talking about the possible consequences of inaction. Take your cues from what the person says — for example, "What happened the last time you stopped taking medicine your doctor prescribed?"

Communication Barriers

Good listening isn't without its challenges. Many of us engage in several habits that will make active listening difficult to accomplish in a conversation. Following roadblocks to communication can stop the communication altogether.

Roadblocks To Communication

- *"Why"* questions. Such questions tend to make people defensive.

- Quick reassurance works, saying things like, *"Don't worry about that."*

- Giving specific advice because it changes the dynamic of the conversation. E.g., *"I think it would be best for you to move out to the assisted living."*

- Digging deep for information and forcing someone to talk about things they would rather not discuss.

- Patronising, because it makes the other person feel pitied. E.g., *"You poor thing, I know just how you feel."*

- Preaching, because it makes you the expert in the situation. E.g., *"You should..." Or, "You shouldn't..."*

- Interrupting, because it shows that you aren't really interested in what the other person is actually saying.

The Art of Questioning

The art of teaching relies significantly on effective questioning techniques. We believe that questions have the potential to actually change the classrooms & strengthen students' involvement. Through questions, students become thinkers and learn the important traits of observation, critical analysis, flexibility, and creativity.

There are four major types of questions which help a teacher initiate, expand, or conclude the discussions.

Major Types of Question Categories

- **Open-ended Questions:** Teachers use open-ended questions to expand the discussion — for example, begin with: "How? What? Where? Who? Which?" For example, "When she said that to you, how did that make you feel?"

- **Reflective Questions:** These can help students understand more about what they said — for example, someone tells you, "I'm tensed I won't remember." A good reflective question might be, "It sounds like you would like some help remembering, or you're concerned about your memory in the future?"

- **Leading Questions:** Leading questions can sometimes be helpful but often suggest that you know better than the person you're talking to or are trying to get specific information from the other person — you are leading the conversation (rather than letting them lead). You should avoid asking too many of these types of questions when engaged in active listening. For example, "Would you like to talk about it?" "What happened then?" "Could you tell me more?"

- **Closed-Ended Questions:** Close-ended questions can usually be answered with a single word. They don't lead to more information but can make a person feel more defensive (as though the conversation is more of an interrogation than a give-and-take). Avoid these questions. Use closed-ended questions to prompt for specifics — for example, lead with: "Is? Are? Do? Did? Can? Could? Would?" For example, "Would you like an apple?"

2.4. Simple Conversation Courtesies

Use these courtesies to try and keep the conversation going or to interrupt the flow to help focus on a specific topic or gain clarity on a topic.

- *"Excuse me/Pardon me...."*

- *"One moment please/Just a second...."*

- *"Let's talk about solutions."*

- *"May I suggest something?"*

EFFECTIVE CLASSROOM COMMUNICATION

Teachers who understand the dynamics of effective communication aspire to adjust their language to improve input for their learners; by doing so, they make communication more comprehensible and usable for their learners.

There are diversified challenges that teachers tackle in the classroom. Some of them are listed below.

- Correcting errors and offering suggestions

- Assessing progress and participation

- Maintaining classroom discipline and enforcing rules.

- Guiding student interpersonal relationships during group work, pair work, and whole-class activities

- Nurturing students' confidence as they learn new content and skills

- Motivating students to progress and develop autonomous learning habits

- Planning and managing learning experiences for students with diverse learning styles, personalities, maturity levels, and self-regulation abilities

Facing all of these intricate tasks, along with the pressures of time and limited resources, it is no wonder that teachers can become exhausted and frustrated at times. However, even in times of frustration, we must work to maintain a positive learning environment and remember that our students' opinions and feelings must be treated with care. Teachers can do this not only by establishing routines and rules but also with the classroom language, verbal and non-verbal, used to communicate with students.

Approaches To Handle Challenges Of Classroom Communication

Teachers' words can have long-lasting effects on learners. Everyone, regardless of age or background, appreciates being spoken to in an encouraging and positive way. This is not to say that teachers should over-praise students – something they will surely notice and view as insincere – but that they should look for ways to reframe (rephrase or restate) negative language they might be tempted to use as positive statements.

Classroom language, even when you are enforcing rules, should encourage students to choose positive behaviours and demonstrate that teachers believe they can make such choices. For example, what difference do you see between the following statements?

- Everyone, stop talking now. Sit down!
  (Teacher claps hands and looks angry)

- We'll begin once everyone is seated and quiet.
  (Teacher silently waits with a positive expression on her face and looks expectantly at students)

Students who regularly feel insecure, embarrassed, or angered by a teacher's communication style aren't learning effectively. Teachers' voice tone, words, and body language play a critical role in fostering positive classroom rapport, mutual respect, and trust.

Reframing or rephrasing sentences to bring positivity and optimism to the classroom lays a solid foundation for a psychologically safe environment. It boosts the confidence of the learners and helps establish a deeper connection with the teacher.

Some examples given below are adapted from Sally White's 2014 webinar, "Reframing: The Power of Positive Language," part of the Shaping the Way We Teach English webinar series by The Bureau of Educational and Cultural Affairs, US Department of State.

Re-frame Statements & Words to Focus on The Positive

Negative – Deficiency Focus	Positive – Constructive Focus
Problem	Challenge
Impatient	Excited, Enthusiastic, Eager
You're working too slowly. Hurry up.	Everyone is working carefully and being thorough, but we only have 5 minutes left to finish.
Manish, don't be late again! You'll be in big trouble.	Manish, be on time, please. What happens if you are late more than three times? (Prompt the student to supply the consequence)
Prateek, stop interrupting Neha	Prateek, please look at our classroom rules chart. Do we listen quietly while others are speaking?

Appropriate Approach to Correct or Praise Students

☒ Everyone, calm down…behave.

☑ Everyone, please return to your seats, sit quietly, and put your pencils and pens down.

☒ Jenny, I like the way you are behaving.

☑ Jenny, thank you for waiting for your turn to speak. You are being very patient.

☒ There is too much talking going on. Pay attention.

☑ We'll continue when everyone is quiet, and ready to listen to Sara.

Appropriate Body Language & Tone of Voice

Project positivity with relaxed, open body language. Use a calm, warm, and professional tone of voice that is age-appropriate for our students. Speak in an authentic way even if you slow your speech rate down a bit for lower levels.

Examples that Reflect Negative & Positive Body Language

☒ Scowling and frowning, rolling your eyes to be dismissive, throwing your hands up in the air to show frustration, crossing your arms over your chest or tapping your foot to indicate impatience pointing the finger at someone while correcting them.

☑ Smiling, maintaining a calm and neutral face while enforcing rules, relaxing your arms and shoulders, and nodding to indicate agreement or encouragement.

Never Use "Baby Talk," "Sugary" Language, or a Condescending Tone

☒ Oh, sweetie, you are doing such a super, great, wonderful job.

☑ Reet, good job - you used five new vocabulary words in your homework assignment.

Don't be Sarcastic. It is not Funny & Hurts Students' Feelings

☒ Arushi, what part of "Stop talking" did you not understand?

☑ Arushi, it is time to listen now.

Appropriate Approach for Lower Proficiency Level Students

For classroom management purposes, students at lower levels may be able to best understand shorter, imperative statements, but teachers can convey the information with a warm tone and supporting gestures. Using a positive tone and positive body language is especially important with these learners, who may be extra self-conscious about making mistakes and not understanding what their teacher wants.

Ways to Enhance Verbal or Visual Language Inputs by a Teacher in a Classroom

- Speaking at a slower rate for slow learners or beginners and at a normal rate for advanced learners.
- Use repetitions and gestures
- Use stress, intonation, and pauses to emphasise critical aspects
- Avoid idioms, jargon, and slang, as they might create ambiguity and break the flow.
- Paraphrase, reiterate, and summarise learners' responses.
- Using multiple sources of communication, such as
- Adding visual or audio inputs to written text
- Peer tutoring
- Paired talk or reading
- Movies, videos, internet sites and other technological interventions

The success of any classroom is measured by its level of engagement. Effective engagement is the combined result of communication and connection. As teachers, we shall aspire and look for ideas and techniques to improve classroom communication and build deeper connections with our learners.

4

RESOURCES
CREATE, PLAN & MANAGE

Great teachers engineer learning experiences that put students in the driver's seat and then get out of the way.

— Ben Johnson

Teachers have this onus on them to identify and analyse the needs of learners, demands of lessons and resources available to meet the objectives. From walls and windows of the classrooms to the textbooks and learners themselves, all are potential resources available to teachers most of the time. Planning and tracking the resources is vital for designing rich learning experiences for our learners. Effective teachers design and deliver lessons that promote the development of learning and thinking strategies. Designing a well-knit lesson plan is an indicator of the high level of teacher efficiency and the best utilisation of all the available resources or resources created for the lesson delivery.

Napoleon Hill stated, "Plan your work and work your plan." The deep-set meaning of this simple yet profound statement tells us that if we want our plan to be materialised, we need to pre-plan it. Every profession demands this professionalism from its people to devote exclusive and enough time to plan before execution. In all situations, we as humans equip ourselves with traits, materials or values that help us navigate our way across. If we are in the teaching profession, we usually prefer to sharpen our axes before reaching the classroom.

In our experience of observing classes of teachers in schools, success at the pedagogical transaction of the content is indicated by the quality and quantity of time invested in the lesson planning process.

Teachers whom we found most effective were those who had-

• An exclusively designed lesson plan.

• Engaging and interesting TLM (Teaching Learning Material)

- Energiser/Opening activity with a list of prompts.

- Inclusive strategies for diversified learners.

- Various forms of assessment.

  And it all starts and proceeds with effective planning of resources.

PLANNING THE CONTENT

Well begun is half done - is how I should put the work culture of Jasmine D'Souza, an exemplary primary teacher who has contributed to the growth of her students through sustained, dedicated hard work and meticulous lesson planning. She strongly believes that classroom teaching should be purpose-driven and not situation driven; thus, she plans her lesson well in advance to take charge of the situation and steer it towards the purpose. Planning the lesson well in advance equips and empowers her to ponder and reflect on the expected situations and available resources to make her class move as anticipated.

According to Jasmine, a teachers' quiver should always be well equipped with tools to engage the students in a productive, joyful and constructive way. A physical form of the mental planning of the content to be delivered is seen in the form of a Lesson Plan (LP).

A well-constructed lesson plan:

- Empowers teachers to enter the classroom with clarity and confidence.

- Helps teachers to integrate interesting and innovative activities to make learning engaging and enjoyable.

- Integrate practices to create a friendly and supportive atmosphere.

- Serves as a tool to track the progress.

- Helps to make the lesson inclusive to cater to varied learning preferences and individual needs.

- Enables teacher to make best of the class time.

However, let us also admit that despite such minute planning of different components of a successful class, there would still be instances where the teacher would need to tweak the content on the spot as per the need of the situation. Here lies the teacher's expertise, her passion for her profession, and her love for all her students.

Teachers can guide students to a lesson's essential learning and content more efficiently if teachers and students are both aware of the important outcomes of the learning experience.

(The 6 Principles for exemplary teaching of English Learners, Grades K-12, TESOL 2018, PP 44)

Key Considerations While Planning the Lesson

Lesson planning is both a skill and an art. Teachers who are adept at designing effective lesson plans keep Content Objectives and Learning Strategies as the main focus areas. Levine & McCosekey has enlisted a set of a questions that a teacher may ask while formulating content objectives or determing learning strategies.

To formulate content objectives, ask these questions:

- What specifically do I need my students to know or do with the informational content by the end of the lesson?

- Is my objective grade appropriate?

- Is it mapped to the learning outcomes recommended by the state curriculum?

- Is my objective challenging for my students?

- How can I communicate the objectives to my students?

- Is my objective measurable?

- What contextual support can I provide for maximised learning?

To determine learning strategy objectives, ask these questions:

- What learning strategy will I use or demonstrate to help my students learn more efficiently?

- Is my strategy doable and measurable?

- Is it age and grade-appropriate?

- How can I communicate my objectives to my students? (Levine & McCosekey, 2013)

Every lesson plan irrespective of the grade, the content, the context or strategies to be integrated has 6 major components and follow a basic formula or hierarchy as explained below.

The Basic Lesson Plan Formula

1. **Preview:** Giving learners an overview of the day's lesson conveys a definite purpose and plan behind the day's activities. (This step may be done either before or after any warm-up activities.)

2. **Warm-Up:** Just as a concert often starts with a short, lively piece to warm the audience up, a lesson often starts with a brief activity that is relatively lively. Its main function is to generate a good class atmosphere, but it can also be used to review previous lessons or introduce new material in the day's lesson. Incidentally, the warm-up tends to set the tone for the lesson. If it involves real communication, it will reinforce the importance of genuine communication right from the beginning of the period.

3. **Main Activities:** These are the main course of the day's menu, the more demanding activities to which most of the lesson will be devoted.

4. **Optional Activity:** This is an activity you hope to use but are ready to omit if there is a shortage of time. (Generally, I designate one of my main activities as optional by marking it if time permits in my lesson plan.)

5. **Reserve (or spare-tire) Activity:** This activity is not an integral part of your lesson plan but is available in case the other parts of the lesson go more quickly than you planned, leaving you with spare time to fill.

6. **Closing:** End the lesson by quickly reviewing/reemphasising one or more main points of the lesson and assigning homework. How might this formula be applied to a specific lesson?

Teachers must devise ways and methods to communicate their learning objectives with their learners. Simply telling students about the learning objectives may not be sufficient for many learners. It is always preferable to write the objectives down, read them aloud, and then demonstrate what a successful outcome might look or sound like (Echevarria, Vogt, & Short, 2017).

It is always helpful to show examples, such as a sample essay, a poster, or an exhibit of the eventual outcome of the content objective in a unit.

Lesson Planning: Formats & Templates

There are as many ways to structure a lesson plan as there are different teaching situations, and no single plan can serve as a model for all situations. Every effective lesson plan follows a format that identifies learning outcomes, objectives, teaching methods, and assessment as the essential elements of any T-L process.

Lesson plan formats can vary in their names, but the core elements of any lesson plan remain the same. Any lesson plan must begin with activating the prior knowledge or preparing learners or exploring their previous knowledge and shall go through a presentation or explanation of the topic and conclusion through assessment or evaluation. Various organisations and teachers have been using different formats or templates to structure their plans for the lesson to be taught and transacted. Throughout our teaching and mentoring experiences, we have used and recommended several lesson plan formats and have seen teachers using a myriad of formats to plan their classroom practices. Personally, out of all, the 4A, 4P, and 5E lesson plan formats have been the easiest and most comprehensive formats for planning the lessons.

All these formats are named after the first letter of the stages they follow.

4A Stands for			
Activate Prior Knowledge	Acquire New Knowledge	Application	Assessment

4P Stands for			
Prepare	Present	Practice	Perform

5E Stands for				
Engage	Explore	Explain	Elaborate	Evaluate

A teacher may use any of the above formats, as each format gives the opportunity to arrange the objectives and resources according to various stages of the lesson delivery. For the sake of reference and better understanding, we have elaborated on the 4A lesson format and have given sample lessons for 4P and 5E formats.

4A LESSON PLANNING

4A lesson plan format provides an outline for mastering concepts and real-world examples. It is a systematic and structured approach to make students ready to learn, make important connections to past learning and prepare their brains for new content. New content is presented, taught, and applied to real-world or past situations. Finally, an assessment is given to determine student understanding. Let's dig a bit deeper into these components.

Activating Prior Knowledge

What does it mean to activate prior knowledge, and how can teachers accomplish this? The term simply refers to tapping into a student's previous experience with the topic. For example, suppose the new learning is about oceanic life. In that case, a teacher could activate students' prior knowledge by connecting to other life forms they have studied or asking students to share experiences about the ocean.

In fact, many instructional methods can be used to activate prior knowledge, including:
- Brainstorming
- Games
- Journaling
- Conversations
- Concept Mapping

Acquire New Knowledge

During this instructional time, teachers promote higher-order thinking and prompt students to use inquiry skills in order to master content. Why do this? Instead of a serve-and-return method of instruction, which simply has students listen and repeat content, the 4-A model fosters a more rigorous learning model, with students thinking deeply about the content. This is accomplished in countless ways, such as having guest speakers, using interactive learning logs, role-playing, and teaching mini-lessons. This is the typical 'instructional methods' portion of lesson plans with an emphasis on pushing towards high-level skills.

For one lesson in oceanic life study, a teacher may have students watch a video of life in the ocean and then read about how mammals and fish interact to survive. Another day she may have a zoologist speak to the students and then have students respond to the experience by writing a letter asking further questions.

Application

During this portion of the 4-A plan, teachers plan for ways students can take in the new information, consolidate it, and apply it in new and valuable ways. Students apply their knowledge by sharing their ideas, creating a product, participating in activities, doing a case study, and so on.

It is at this stage where the real action or learning by doing happens. During this phase, the teacher provides opportunities for group work, collaborative assignments, and tasks to students. Students work in pairs, in small groups or individually to apply the knowledge gained from the session. It is a highly dynamic phase; thus, a teacher should take up the role of a facilitator and ensure the availability of the resources required. Seating arrangements are also modified for effective group works.

Assessment

It is the final and the most critical part of the 4-A lesson plan. Here the teacher plans

OCEANIC LIFE LESSON PLAN

Objective

Students will be able to explain the relationship between mammals and fish in oceanic life.

Activate Prior Knowledge

Students will do a 3-2-1 experience in writing, then share with group
3 things they know about ocean life,
2 things they want to know
1 thing they are confused about.

Acquire New Knowledge

Watch video about oceanic life; read follow-up article. Divide students into two groups mammals and fish. Ask Group to find ways they interact with the other group, Then partners students to have conversation about their interaction as fish/mammals.

Application

Student partners present information on chart paper to the group, then synthesise as a class to create a final product of Mammal/fish interactions.

Assessment

as an exit slip, students create a new 3-2-1; 3 things they learned, 2 things they could teach, 1 thing they are still confused about.

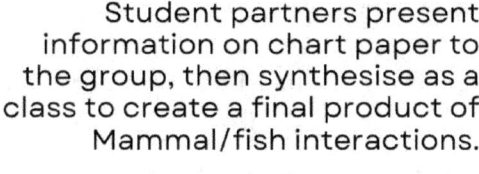

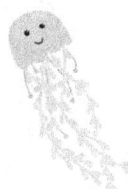

Source:www.study.com

and executes ways and methods to check the level of understanding and competence developed through the teaching and learning process. For oceanic life, the teacher has used the 3-2-1 method for quick assessment with the help of an exit slip. In the last leg of the lesson, all the students are instructed to fill out the exit slip with the following three prompts.

3 Things they have learnt	2 Things they could teach	1 Thing they are still confused about

The teacher may also use strategies like KWL charts, Frayer's Model and applications like Kahoot, Nearpod, Padlet, Mentimeter etc., to check for understanding and response. Teachers who go the extra mile also opt for techniques like Peer assessment, Self-assessment and surprise assessments to make evaluation more effective and stress-free.

4P LESSON PLANNING

This format of lesson planning was first introduced to us as a part of our professional development training by TESOL, sponsored by the US Embassy and SCERT Delhi. It was a blended training of 6 months with teaching practicum. For teaching practicum, we had to design, develop and deliver lessons for teaching of English. The lesson plan format suggested to us was PPPP. It is an easy, logical and sequential approach to design an all-inclusive effective lesson plan.

Each P of PPPP model represents a stage of the lesson. Starting from Preparing students for the session to selecting most suitable mediums for Presentation, the lesson plan offers opportunities to Practice the learnings and finally assessing them on the basis of their Performance.

The PPPP template shared with us during the training is shared below for your quick reference. A print and use template is also appended in the Teacher's Activity Book The 4P lesson plan is of great importance for teacher trainers to design and plan workshops. It helps you to structure and stack all the resources and references to be used for the session.

Recently, a 03 hour workshop on Gamification was delivered to a group of pre service teachers and the whole session was designed using PPPP format. The same lesson plan is given below as an illustration. Taking ideas from the sample plan and using the blank template you can easily design and effectively deliver an effective lesson easily and quickly.

SAMPLE LESSON PLAN: PPPP Format

Workshop on Gamification in Learning for D.EL.Ed 2nd Year Students

Name of the facilitator/s: **Karamjeet Singh**
Grade/Language Level: **Pre-Service/Intermediate**

Lesson topic: **Gamification**
Lesson Duration: **03 hours**

OVERALL OBJECTIVES

- Develop an understanding of games for learning and Gamification of learning

- Playing and creating collaborative board games

- Identify and elaborate upon elements of Gamification

- Understand and experience Gamification of learning

4P LESSON PLAN

STAGE	Est. Time	Activities Planned	Resources/ Actions Required
PREPARE	30 min	• Introduction • Group Formation • Games	• Game Pictures • Group Formation • Group Printout • Chart/A4 Sheets
PRESENT - Part - 1	30 min	• Elements of the Game • Group Presentation • Gallery Pasting	• Chart Papers • Markers • Group Discussion
PRESENT - Part - 2	30 min	• Board Games • Rotating Learning Stations • Group Sharing	• Board Games - 1/group • Dice - 1/group • Instructions to Play
PRACTICE - Part - 1	45 min	• Creating Board Games • Gallery Pasting	• Chart/A4 Sheets • Sketch pens/markers • Instructions
PRACTICE - Part - 2	30 min	• Word Chain • Voca Bingo • Finding Words	• Black/ White Board • Tissue Papers • Markers/ Chalks
PERFORM	15 min	• Gallery Walk • Feedback Form • Individual Score Card • Exit Ticket	• Google Form • Score Card Template • Slips • Box

5E LESSON PLANNING

This lesson plan format was taught to us during our LIC (Learning Improvement Cycles) workshop for mentors and TDCs (Teacher Development Co-ordinator). We cascaded this lesson planning method to more than 50K teachers teaching at government schools of Delhi. The 5E lesson planning has 5 sequential stages with each stage starting from letter E. The lesson begins with Engaging learners in generating their interest and tapping their previous knowledge. Teacher being in the role of a facilitator provides resources and opportunities to learners for Exploring the key concepts. Students are encouraged to Explain their observations and findings followed by Elaboration/Extension by the teacher and finally students are Evaluated on the basis of their performance. This format provides ample opportunities for bringing learner's autonomy and collaborative learning.

CSCOPE, an organization that works for curriculum development, has created a 5E model of instruction that gives a detailed elaboration of each stage with role of teacher and students at each stage. (Refer to the image on the next page)

During the first lockdown of covid-19, it was the need of the hour to orient and train teachers of government schools about online teaching and learning applications. To train thousands of teachers for digital and blended teaching methods in a structured manner, we designed and delivered lesson plans using the 5E model.

All the stages of the lesson are divided under 03 broad categories viz. Opening Activity (Engage), Main Activity (Explore, Explain, Elaborate), and Closing Activity (Evaluate). Shared below is the same lesson plan sample for your ready reference.

Content as a Resource: Organising and Presenting

Information transacted during the lesson needs to be retained, reproduced and recalled by the learners. Teachers must come up with interesting ways to organise and present the information that makes it easy for students to compile their learning in the most concise and presentable form. There are ways of organising information visually to help students understand and remember it. These are tools that let learners make connections, create a plan, and communicate effectively. A good organiser simplifies complex information and lays it out in a way that makes it easier for learners to understand and assimilate. Graphic organisers may include images and text, depending on the purpose and the students' preferred learning style.

The 5E Model of Instruction

5E Definition	Teacher Behavior	Student Behavior
Engage		
• Generate interest • Access prior knowledge • Connect to past knowledge • Set parameters of the focus • Frame the idea	• Motivates • Creates interest • Taps into what students know or think about the topic • Raises questions and encourages responses	• Attentive in listening • Ask questions • Demonstrates interest in the lesson • Responds to questions demonstrating their own entry point of understanding
Explore		
• Experience key concepts • Discover new skills • Probe, inquire, and question experiences • Examine their thinking • Establish relationships and understanding	• Acts as a facilitator • Observes and listens to students as they interact • Asks good inquiry-oriented questions • Provides time for students to think and to reflect • Encourages cooperative learning	• Conducts activities, predicts, and forms hypotheses or makes generalizations • Becomes a good listener • Shares ideas and suspends judgment • Records observations and/or generalizations • Discusses tentative alternatives
Explain		
• Connect prior knowledge and background to new discoveries • Communicate new understandings • Connect informal language to formal language	• Encourages students to explain their observations and findings in their own words • Provides definitions, new words, and explanations • Listens and builds upon discussion form students • Asks for clarification and justification • Accepts all reasonable responses	• Explains, listens, defines, and questions • Uses previous observations and findings • Provides reasonable responses to questions • Interacts in a positive, supportive manner
Extend/Elaborate		
• Apply new learning to a new or similar situation • Extend and explain concept being explored • Communicate new understanding with formal language	• Uses previously learned information as a vehicle to enhance additional learning • Encourages students to apply or extend the new concepts and skills • Encourages students to use terms and definitions previously acquired	• Applies new terms and definitions • Uses previous information to probe, ask questions, and make reasonable judgments • Provides reasonable conclusions and solutions • Records observations, explanations, and solutions
Evaluate		
• Assess understanding (Self, peer and teacher evaluation) • Demonstrate understanding of new concept by observation or open-ended response • Apply within problem situation • Show evidence of accomplishment	• Observes student behaviors as they explore and apply new concepts and skills • Assesses students' knowledge and skills • Encourages students to assess their own learning • Asks open-ended questions	• Demonstrates an understanding or knowledge of concepts and skills • Evaluates his/her own progress • Answers open-ended questions • Provides reasonable responses and explanations to events or phenomena

Based on the 5E Instructional Model presented by Dr. Jim Barufaldi at the Eisenhower Science Collaborative Conference in Austin, Texas, July 2002.

5E LESSON PLAN

Lesson Elements	What Does It Look Like?	What Tools Can I use?
OPENING ACTIVITY:		
Engage:	• Brainstorm • Access Prior Knowledge • Ask Questions	
MAIN ACTIVITIES:		
Explore	• Watch Videos • Read Articles • Research • Discuss	
Explain	• Instruction • Modelling • Scaffolding	
Elaborate	• Make connections between concepts to real life. • Apply learning to new situations • Explain how & why	
CLOSING ACTIVITY:		
Evaluate	• Formative Assessment • Reflections	

Graphic Organisers: An Effective Way to Organize Information

To use GOs most efficiently, provide students with pre-printed organisers or encourage them to draw their own. Either way, teach students to use them by modelling the behaviour first. Consider making anchor charts for so students can refer back to them as they work.

With younger students, make them understand how to choose specific types of organisers depending on their goals. For instance, students taking notes while studying may find a concept map most helpful. A Venn diagram or T chart is the best choice when comparing two topics.

Jill Stake, in his article on effective uses of GOs, enlists a large number of interesting and easy-to-use graphic organisers with a brief explanation for teachers.

Story Map

This is one of the first organisers many kids learn to use. Story maps are simple for little ones, laying out the setting, characters, beginning, middle, and end. Older students can expand the map to add more details.

Timelines

Timelines are mostly used in history and social studies classes, though they can be helpful while reading books too.

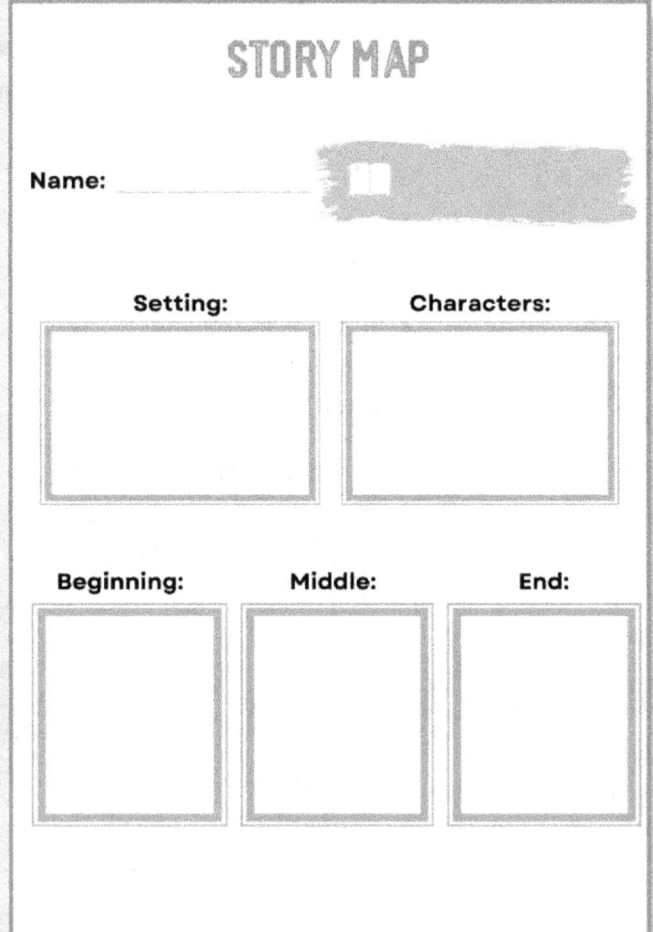

Sequencing Organisers

Sequencing organisers are generally used to lay out the steps of a procedure or a science experiment.

SEQUENCING ORGANIZERS

Topic: ....
　　By: ....

First: ....
....
....

Next: ....
....
....

Then: ....
....
....

Last: ....
....
....

KWL Chart

KWL (What I Know, What I Wonder, What I Learned) charts are a great way to help kids think about what they want to learn about a topic and give them the onus for actually finding out that information. The first column is a list of everything they already know. The second column lists what they would like to learn, and the third one provides new information acquired along the way.

KWL CHART

Topic:

K What I Know	W What I Wonder	L What I Learned

Idea Web

Idea webs are used when there's a lot of information to remember about a subject, and it is a great way to organise it all. Learners can explore a subject rather than just making a list or taking notes, and it is more likely to help kids actually remember the information.

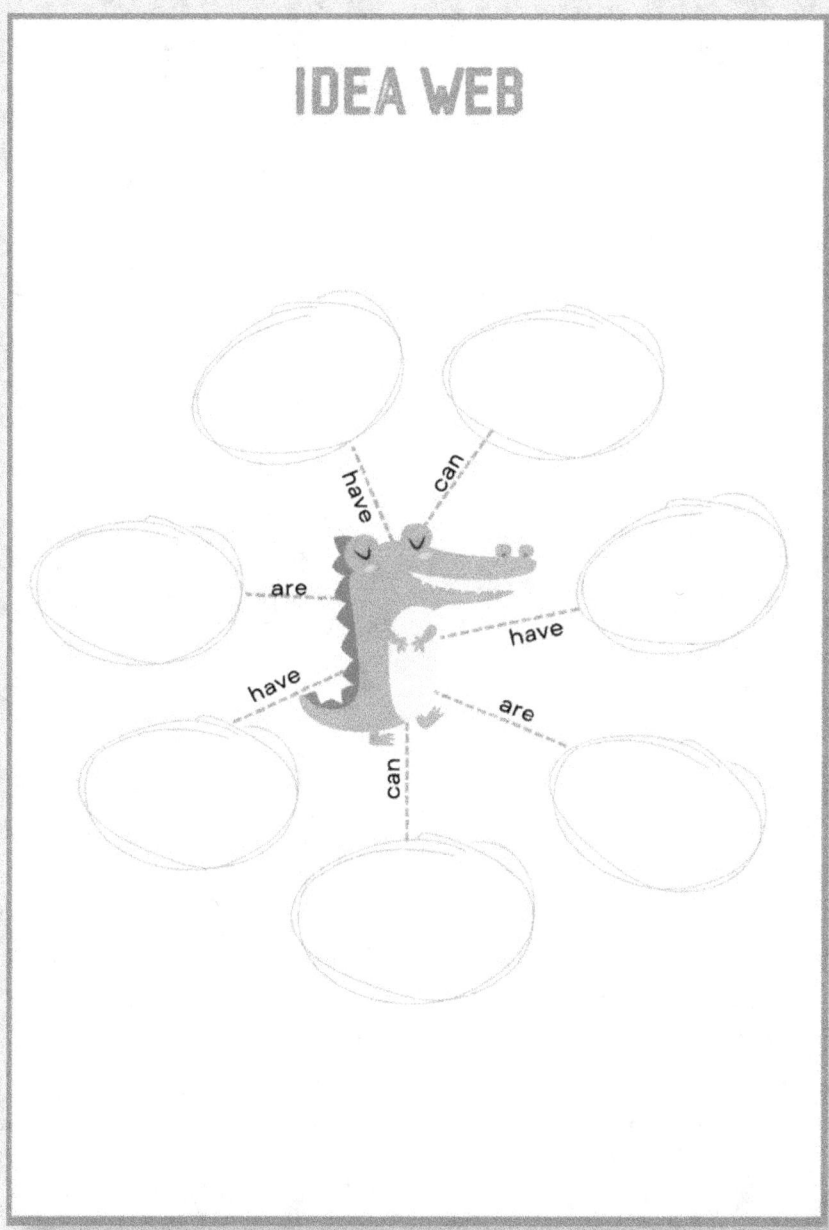

FRAYER S MODEL

Definition	Characteristics

Examples	Non-Examples

Frayer's Model

The Frayer Model is a graphic organiser that helps students clarify the meaning of unfamiliar vocabulary words they come across while listening, reading, and viewing texts. They can be effectively used before reading to activate background knowledge, during reading to monitor vocabulary, or after reading to assess vocabulary. This model is a simple but useful tool that serves the purpose of a graphic organiser. It is a way for students who need a multisensory approach to put a concept in a visual format.

It has a lot of uses but is most often applied to vocabulary. The term is mentioned in the centre, with four sections surrounding it for definition, characteristics, examples, and non-examples. There could also be sections for definition, synonyms, illustration, and using the term in a sentence.

PLANNING THE CONNECT

"Let not culture create us; let the culture be created by us."

Every teacher dream and desire to have a class that is cheerful and offers a conducive environment for effective co-learning. A teacher can create a progressive & collaborative culture by leveraging various routines, rituals and human emotions in the classroom.

Creating Classroom Culture of Recognition and Appreciation

As a basic human tendency, all of us feel happy upon contribution and when we feel valued. Classrooms where efforts are recognised and achievements are appreciated usually are the most positive and connected classrooms.

A culture of recognition is created through small acts and gestures of acknowledging the efforts and actions of the learners.

Recognition can be seen as a simple act of marking and commenting upon the work in the notebooks, or it can also be a simple smile and nodding of the head in affirmation. Appreciation can also be seen as a pat on the back by the teacher or a round of applause by the whole class.

Ideas for Creating a Culture of Recognition and Appreciation

Certificates & Badges

Teachers and administrators who believe in giving certificates to learners, realize the significance of this small, signed, thick paper and use it to boost morale and improve the level

When asked, what goes into creating a classroom culture of recognition and appreciation, Ms. Mamta Saikia, CEO Bharti Foundation, quotes

"It is important that classrooms encourage all the students to find their potential including the shy ones."

She supports her statement with some of the concrete examples and experiences she had at ground level in various government schools as well as schools run by Bharti Foundation.

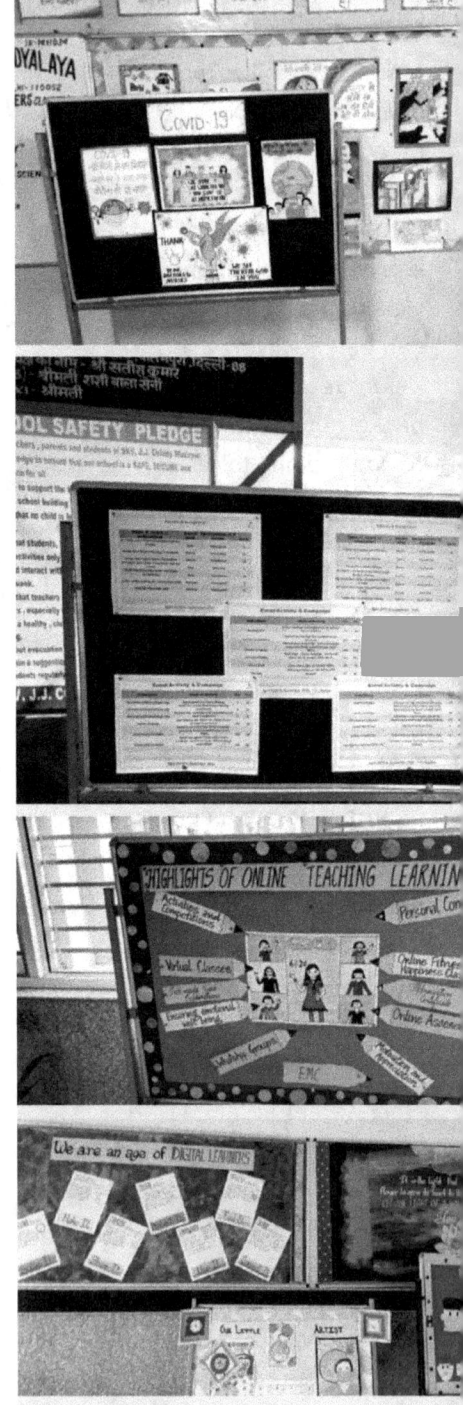

Gallery Walk: Images of Initiatives taken by Bharti Foundations displayed in corridor of a government school of Delhi

of participation of the learners. While certifying the students, we shall consider the following:

- Certify not only those who have performed but also those who have attended, participated and completed the course/training/project/event

- Certify not only the toppers but also those who have struggled hard to improve their results.

- Certify publicly to honour and appreciate the efforts and engagement of the learners.

- Badges for different roles and outstanding performances shall be given to students.

- Applications like Autocrat, certify "em, Canva, Adobe Illustrator etc., can be used to make beautiful and customised certificates easily and freely.

The Bharti Foundation has been transforming schools and classroom processes to bring more cheer and joy in the classrooms. Many initiatives have been taken in the schools of various state governments and results have been phenomenal. Introducing culture of clubs, recognition of talents, and bringing community and schools together are some of the many programs that ensures quality, innovation and meaningful engagement. "School Friend Badges" is one such unique and effective initiative followed by more than 170 Satya Bharti Schools situated in different states of India.

To recognize efforts, reward achievements, and spread awareness, Bharti Foundation has started gallery walks in the schools. In this unique initiative, schools are advised to display their activities, achievements, and achievers in the school corridors. These corridors then act like an exhibition gallery showcasing the events and initiatives of the schools. It not only infuses the school, the students and the teachers with confidence and pride but also helps visitors to have a glimpse of activities that take place in school.

Awards & Trophies

The physical manifestation of appreciation comes in the form of awards or trophies given to deserving students (Be well aware of the definition of the word-well deserved). Do you remember having received an award for

- The Most Regular Student
- The Most Well-Dressed Student
- The Most Well-Behaved Student
- Ms. Perfectionist or Mr. Perfectionist
- Mr. Friendliest and many more such titles, which are not very conventional titles to hear.

Mementos, trophies, medals and awards are those things of beauty which are a joy forever. These are the symbols of achievements and honour to be cherished forever. Winning them, holding them, and displaying them infuses us with pride and energy.

Let's have a camaraderie of trust and fondness growing in our organisation where there is a genuine reason for everyone to feel happy and confident, where you understand that not only are you watched for your major expected actions but also for seemingly insignificant contributions.

Assembly Appreciation

School days turn everyone nostalgic, early morning school assembly and the Principal showering appreciation on students who have brought laurels to the school in various inter and intra-school activities. A great morning kick starts well when the cheers and thunderous applause for our fellow mates fill and echo in the school premises. The wide smiles and the twinkle in the eyes of the deserving students are worth a watch!

Special Events Invitation

We have seen the culture in our schools changing very rapidly for the better. Now all stakeholders realise the importance of the pivot of our schools and our students, following the policy of NCLB (No Child Left Behind). All students are understood to come in an exclusive and elusive package of uniqueness. A sensible and sensitive human being shall maintain his humility and give the much-required time to his students whether it means taking lunch with them or sipping tea at the school premises.

Classroom Celebrations

An activity that encourages students to honour their peers helps build a strong classroom community. Students celebrate each other for no other reason than being a member of the community.

Celebrations bring the children closer to each other's cultural beliefs and traditions to develop respect and understanding for each other.

Some of the ideas to motivate and celebrate students are listed below:

Motivating Students & Celebrating Student Success in the Classroom

- Verbal Praise...
- Write a Note...

- Send a Note/ Email/ Text to a Parent or Guardian...
- Class Incentives/ Celebrations...
- Teacher's Assistant for the Day...
- Displaying Work in the Classroom...
- Hold an Award Ceremony...

Other Celebration Ideas in the Classroom

- Birthday Celebrations
- Celebrating Festivals
- Celebrating achievements-scholastic or co-scholastic
- Celebration of important days in school such as World water day, Child labour day, Halloween day, Christmas day, Mother's Day, Thanks Giving Day, to name a few.
- Celebration during the beginning of the session and session ending.

PLANNING THE CONTEXT

Context of any classroom is reflected through its daily routines and rituals. A well-informed teacher with a positive mental attitude carefully plans the routines and practice the rituals to make the environment conducive for learning. Given below are some of the ideas we have gathered from our exposures and experiences:

Entry Ritual

The entry ritual is a great strategy to use in classrooms. Classrooms generally get disengaged when students are first entering the classroom in the morning. This technique helps to minimise the loss by adding a fun element daily.

A good way to allow for the enforcement of these behaviours could be by using instrumental conditioning. Instrumental conditioning is a simple way of doing something that will make a behaviour more or less likely to occur. For example: Praising the students that are following the instructions to submit their homework at the beginning of class or those students that immediately begin working on their do now assignment.

Here the students are made to curate their specific and peculiar style for entering the class. The teacher could have a chart at the entry point of the class indicating the different styles students could choose from for registering their entry. It could be creating a face about how they are feeling that day, a high five with the teacher standing to welcome them at the class entry point, a handshake or a punch touch gesture.

Not only does it create a deeper connection between the teacher and the taught by means of physical contact, eye to eye contact, but also passing of a pleasant smile to each other makes the atmosphere very congenial and conducive to receptivity.

Exit Rituals

Common classroom transformations that teachers are facilitating to enhance student engagement are the buzzword for the season. Highly engaging room transformations reignite their excitement for honing their learning abilities.

In this particular topic, we are going to help the teacher and taught gauge the level of involvement, learning, understanding and retention by the students at the end of the period. In a 40-minute class period, students are presented with a lot of information; some bits of information is much more important than others. As a common exit ritual, teachers across the globe use Exit tickets. Wherein the main concepts of the lesson are revised by answering some quick questions or performing certain activities before leaving the class.

Reasons to use Exit Tickets in your Classroom

- You can use the data provided from an exit ticket to reflect on the lesson delivered to differentiate, modify, or redo the teaching pedagogy of a lesson. In a few minutes, at the end of a lesson, students are able to respond to a prompt that will provide them with information that otherwise may have gone unnoticed.
- Ask students to paste their tickets on a traffic light to indicate whether they're doing fine or struggling with understanding the concepts. That way, you can focus on those which students need more assistance with.
- Valuable as they are to teachers, exit tickets are also important for helping students self-assess. This version gives them a chance to reflect on their strengths and areas for improvement.
- Experienced teachers know that a good classroom is more about a back-and-forth, give-and-take model rather than just "teacher talks, students listen." Students are most successful when teachers are constantly assessing their progress and realigning instruction. Exit tickets are one terrific way to get immediate feedback from the students. They work in every classroom at every level. Here are some of our favourite ways to put them into practice.

Examples of Exit Rituals

- **Pose a Lunch Question and Smiley Survey**

In elementary classrooms, there's no need to wait until the end of the day. Teachers have also been using exit tickets just before the lunch or recess period. It can either

Ask "What Stuck With You Today?"

Find out what made the most impact with one simple question. Post-it notes/ Sticky notes are wonderful to be used for exit tickets; Students just have to post theirs to the board on their way out the door.

WHAT STUCK WITH YOU TODAY?

Have them "Tweet" it

This cute "Twitter" board is sure to appeal to young social media fans. You may laminate the cards so they can be reused.

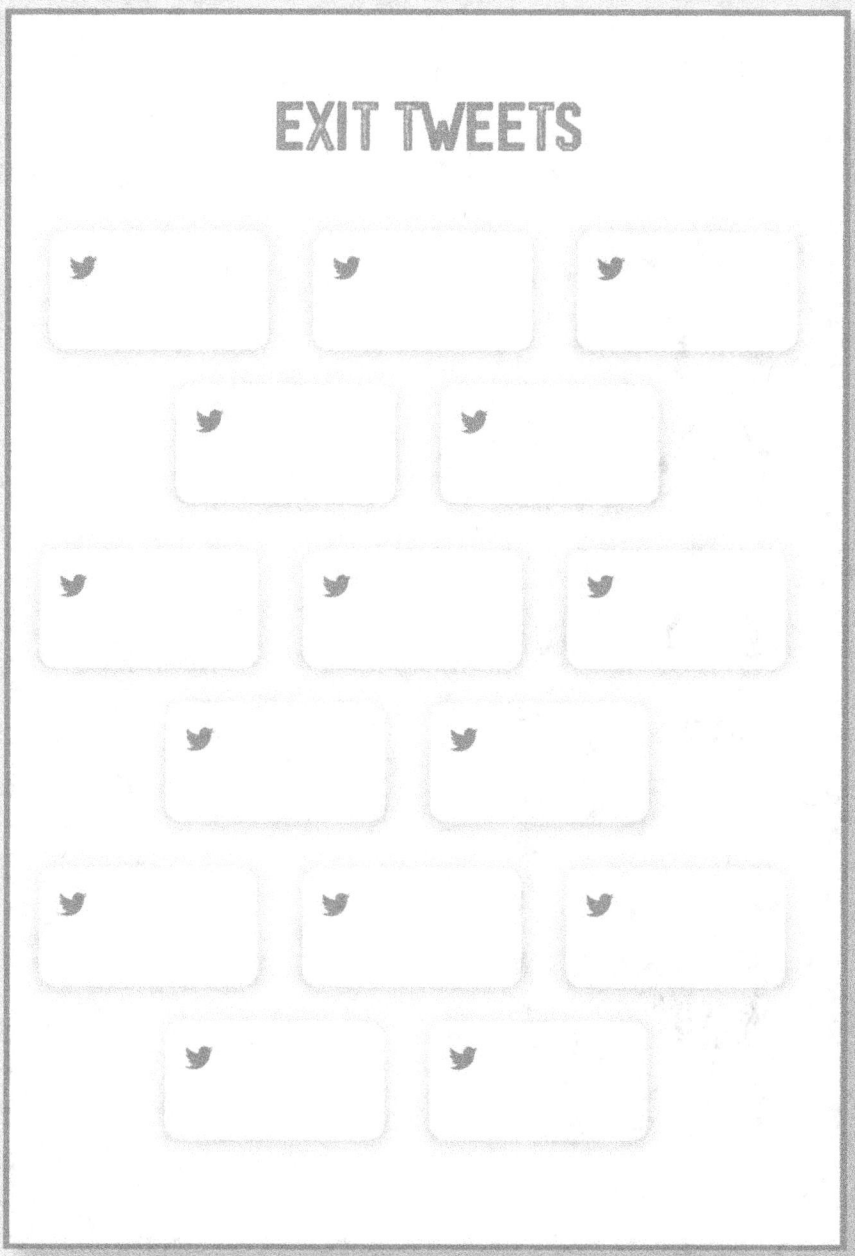

Collect exit tickets on a traffic light

Ask students to post their tickets on a traffic light to signal whether they're doing fine or struggling. That way, you can focus on those who need more help and attention. Sometimes exit tickets are quite specific, but other times you just want to know what their general reaction is to the classroom activities.

TRAFFIC LIGHT

I need more help:

Getting It!

Yes! I can!

Gauge understanding with emojis

Here's a way to help learners connect and share their progress. Ask them to circle an emoji on the free printable and explain how and why it reflects their understanding.

EMOJI EXIT TICKET

Circle the emoji(s) that reflects how you got on today in the lesson. Explain your reasons why...

I chose this emoji because...
....
....

be an academic question, or a simple smiley survey about their well-being and state of mind. Smiley Survey is a simple yet effective way for teachers to have a general assessment of the students mental and psychological state that helps them to design and deliver their lesson in the best possible manner.

Ms. Mamta Saikia also shares her experience with Smiley Survey and proudly quotes,

"Bharti foundation undertook a smiley survey in Satya Bharti school of Bharti Foundation when students came back to schools post COVID. Based on the survey results, teachers undertook engagement activities in the classrooms to energize and motivate students."

Classroom Contract

A classroom contract is built with the participation and ideas from everyone. It is something that everyone willingly adheres to and follows with strong conviction. Everyone shares responsibility for the agreements as they are formulated with mutual consensus. It is also a nice alternative to traditional classroom rules.

We can purposely create a classroom environment of mutual respect and collaboration by establishing and holding all participants accountable to supportive agreements about how they wish to be together. Such agreements like these are co-created along with students.

Things To Keep in Mind While Framing Classroom Contract

- Keep them in affirmative.
- Have short sentences.
- Keep the number of agreements limited to 5-7.
- Flexibility to alter them if a need arises, should be an open proposition.
- Give students the privilege of writing it on a chart paper and putting it up in the class.

No Hands Activity

'No Hands' student selector randomly selects a student's name from a class list for attempting questions or doing an activity in the classroom. It is based on the idea that when a teacher randomly selects pupils to answer questions, all students are more attentive, as anyone in the class may be asked the next question.

As a reality check practice, students connect to this quick and fair way of student selection, and teachers can never be accused of favouritism or giving opportunities to any student too frequently. The process adopted seems fair enough for the students and the teachers alike.

Teachers can make use of Popsicle sticks or Ice cream sticks, as they are popularly called. They are readily available at any stationery shop and don't cost a fortune. After procuring them, the names of all the students in the class need to be written on separate sticks. This pack of sticks is then put in a tumbler or a small box. After posing a prompt or a question to the class, the teacher asks a student to randomly pick up any stick and read the name on it, thereby declaring the name of the child who would be asked to answer the next question.

Once the stick has been used, it would be placed out of the tumbler to allow other students to get a fair enough chance to participate in the questions to follow.

It is important to provide students with scaffolds which they can use when they don't know an answer. This helps to reduce anxiety and also provides a different variant to "I don't know". These question prompts with visuals are to support students who can't read the prompts. We review these questions before every 'No hands up' session, so hopefully, these scaffolds become ingrained in the classroom routine.

Alternate to *"I Don't Know"* could include:

- Can I have a clue?
- Can I have some time to think?
- Can you repeat the question?
- May I ask a friend for help?
- Can you ask that in a different way?
- Can I have more information?
- I'm not sure, but my best guess is…

Equal Participation

Teachers are very special and hold a place of great importance in the lives of every student. Not only do students remember the subject that you taught them but also how you taught it. The way you smile, who all you have eye-to-eye contact with, who do you pat on the back and another little gesture, whose names you remember!

In this case, students look up to teachers for support, guidance and motivation.

So, it is our prime responsibility to live up to this expectation of our students. A sensible and sensitive teacher would ensure that in spite of the time and space crunch in our large-sized classrooms, all students would get an equal chance to be able to share their knowledge and feelings in front of the entire class and get confidence that their teacher listens to them. The fact that every child in the classroom deserves to be equally liked and encouraged by the teacher needs to be emphasised.

> THE GREAT THING ABOUT A CLASSROOM CONTRACT IS THAT IT REMOVES THE TEACHER AS THE SOLE AUTHORITARIAN TO MANAGE BEHAVIOR. IT IS NOW THE RESPONSIBILITY OF ALL STUDENTS TO PARTICIPATE IN MANAGING BEHAVIOR SO THAT THE BEST LEARNING ENVIRONMENT IS FOSTERED.

Students in these classrooms co-exist as members of the classroom community. Together, they create a culture of accountability, learning and inclusivity. A teacher's purpose is not to create students as their own image but to develop students who can create their own image.

This could be made possible by choosing judicious options instead of individual participation like small and large group activities, and representatives of the teams that are the team leaders are asked to be the mouthpiece of their own groups. We can also ensure that all students feel valued and are effectively engaged by delegating responsibilities like a child can be asked to be a timekeeper, Discipline in charge, or scorekeeper, to name a few.

5

TRANS-FORMATION
TRANSFORMING CLASSROOMS FOR A BETTER FUTURE

Effective education is not adding a program or a set of programs to a school. Rather it is a transformation of the culture and life of the school.

— David Berkowitz

Every classroom has its specific dynamics and challenges, which are the building blocks of its environment. Competent teachers identify them and use them effectively to transform the classroom environment. They are well aware and equipped with relevant strategies, ready-to-use tools, required techniques, and recreational teaching methods. They know the art and the science of converting a dull and monotonous classroom into an engaging and joyful one. This chapter brings up some of the highly effective tools and tricks used by such teachers across the globe.

All the strategies mentioned in the chapter can create the desired environment and effective alignment of teacher, learner, and learning in any given context for any given content. A teacher may seek and witness transformation in a classroom in three broad categories:

1	2	3
Infrastructural Transformation	Pedagogical Transformation	Behavioural Transformation

INFRA STRUCTURAL TRANSFORMATION

Thousands of schools in Punjab, India, have been transformed on the foundational principle that colourful, vibrant schools are the prerequisites for joyful and meaningful learning.

Now, schools in Punjab have bright walls, clean toilets, modern classrooms, labs and libraries decorated with slogans and paintings etc. This transformation resulted in increased enrolment and engagement in school. These changes are at the surface and administrative level. Still, teachers have the same opportunity to bring such physical transformations into their classrooms and make their classroom atmosphere more welcoming and uplifting.

Some of the simple ideas that teachers may adopt in their classroom to bring infrastructural or surficial transformations are:

Sitting Arrangements

Teachers may not have the authority to buy suitable desks and tables for the classroom. Still, they always have the power to re-arrange the existing furniture to transform their traditional teaching classroom into a modern facilitation classroom. Turning around alternate desks will turn the classroom into small group workspaces with broad tables for 4 to 6 students to work together. If the space allows, a u-shaped arrangement is the best possible arrangement for a small-sized classroom. It ensures equal attention and increased participation of the students.

Building as a Learning Aid (BaLA)

This is an excellent concept for subconscious and joyful learning through the transformation of walls, floors, ceilings and classroom articles like desks, fans, blackboards, almirahs etc. Teachers usually decorate the classroom walls with slogans, quotes, formulas, principles etc., written or drawn by the learners — some of the different and practical ideas for using the walls, floors, ceilings, etc.

This concept is used extensively and holistically in the schools of Punjab and has transformed the environment significantly. Mr. Amarjeet Singh, teacher at a government school of Mansa (Punjab), a national awardee and state coordinator for BaLA with Punjab Government Educational Model, shares proudly, that, "We have made educational parks, used ceilings for demonstrating universe and solar system, walls for labelled diagrams, colourful images, and slogans etc. These small yet significant changes in the external layer of the school or classroom is the most visible layer, thus we try to fill it with emotions and information. It has made our schools more welcoming and teaching learning processes more engaging."

An article, *"A colourful revolution is sweeping across Punjab schools without a single paisa from govt"* was published by The Print, by Chitleen K. Sethi. In her article, she has shared excerpts and views of teachers from Punjab who have been the reason and witness of this transformational journey.

"The school is a three-dimensional space, and if we are able to use it well, it can give a multiple sensory experience to the student. Students respond so well to colours and drawings. Their observation skills improve and retention increases", says Amarjit Singh, state coordinator for BaLA in Punjab, who teaches at a senior secondary smart school at Boha in Mansa.

A government senior secondary school in a village Jaito, Faridkot, has seven rooms, all of which have been painted to look like a train. The classroom coaches are numbered S1 to S7.

The idea behind the 'train' was to encourage students to move ahead in life and keep moving till their goals are met, and was given by Ralli, who was then a primary school teacher. Once the idea became popular, it was copied in many other schools, and is now called 'Education Express'.

Gurpreet Singh Namdhari, art teacher at a government senior secondary school in Nabha, Patiala, said: **"There is sometimes just enough money to buy the paints. In our school, we and the students have painted the walls ourselves. It took us three months to create the Science City Room. The school has an art gallery too."**

The author has shared that, "Right now, in most schools, the focus is on the walls and playgrounds. But teachers are being encouraged to use other elements as learning aids — the floor, windows, doors, fans, trees and flowers."

"Buildings have immense potential and they are a powerful source of informal and subconscious learnings. Using walls for teaching values, natural sciences, mathematics, vocabulary, lives and messages of exemplary beings etc are just few of the innumerable learnings we can impart by using the building creatively and critically".

Mr. Amarjit Singh, National Awardee Teacher, Government Senior Secondary School Ranghrial, Mansa (Punjab)

e-Library (The Digital Library)
Government Primary School, Ralli
District - Mansa
A school with a difference

The images of transformation shared by Mr. Amarjeet Singh

"A flag-pole can be erected in the ground to demonstrate the sun's movement, three-dimensional shapes to understand the concept of a sphere, square, cube etc. Window grills can be used to teach fractions, doors to show various angles," said Ralli.

"We recently started floor activities to develop mind and limb coordination among the younger children. Step counting, shapes, addition and subtraction, and multiplication tables can be taught using the floor.", adds Rajendra Kumar, spokesperson for Punjab Education Model.

Not only Punjab and Delhi, but buildings and walls have been used extensively and creatively since ages and across the globe. Some of the most effective use of buildings gathered from exposures and interactions are listed below:

Gratitude Wall

Assign a corner or a section of the wall where students and visitors may express their gratitude and feelings in short sentences.

Birthday Wall

A huge tree is drawn on the wall, with a passport-sized photograph of a student as its leaves. The student's name and Date of Birth are written below each leaf. It is a great way to build awareness and connection with the students.

Wall of Fame

This section of the wall highlights and celebrates the achievers of the classrooms. It is updated every week or month.

Students of a govt school in Vada Bhaika village, Faridkot | By special arrangement

Good Deeds Wall/Kindness Wall

In this section of the wall, students write briefly about their acts of kindness and proposals for any collaborative good deeds.

Learning Floors

Using coloured chalks, teachers can convert any floor into a learning game, especially for foundational literacy and numeracy.

Rainbow Fans

Colouring the fans in seven different colours of a rainbow (V.I.B.G.Y.O.R.) not only makes the classroom look vibrant but also teaches the concepts of light and colours.

There can be numerous other ways a teacher can think, brainstorm, or search for ideas to transform their classroom walls into learning and motivational spaces.

Classroom Libraries

A slight shift in approach can lead to excellent results. Bringing the library into the class is one such transformational idea. In pursuit of creating an input-rich environment for young learners to develop a love for reading, a thread is tied on a wall from one point to another and books taken from the library, especially purchased or brought by teachers and learners, are hung on the thread. Each student can pick any book to read and return after reading. These are called Hanging Libraries. Teachers can also use "Mobile Libraries", movable magazine stands to keep and display books for students. Teachers can move these libraries to different rooms, which is a boon for low-resource schools.

Activity Corners

Teachers use old plastic and cardboard boxes to keep materials for games, activities, and collaborative work. All these boxes are stacked and arranged in a corner with the bold caption "My Activity Corner". Students actively participate and contribute to enrich this corner.

PEDAGOGICAL TRANSFORMATION

Changing the teaching methodology can transform the spirit and energy of a classroom. For example, the usual "Chalk n Talk" method, if complemented by I.C.T., can bring significant changes in classroom energy. Using a projector and a laptop to show videos, simulate a complex topic, or play some digital game may create a high level of engagement in the class. Similarly, there may be many other pedagogical interventions that can bring immediate transformation in any classroom; some are enlisted and elaborated.

I.C.T. - Integrated Teaching

These days compatible projectors cum computers like Kyan are used in schools in Delhi. It is quite an easy and handy tool for teachers to transform their traditional classrooms into an ICT-enabled audio-visual equipped classroom. It not only amuses them but also helps them sustain interest and expand their attention span. Teachers have used I.C.T. to integrate simulation, digital games, content-specific videos and infographics, presentations or case studies.

C.A.L. (Computer Assisted Learning) and M.A.L. (Mobile Assisted Learning) have been used extensively by teachers and trainers during and after the Covid-19 pandemic.

Teaching through simulated videos or interactive gaming portals improves the interest and involvement of students.

Significant ICT-Based Interventions Used By Teachers Across The World

- Youtube Videos
- L.M.S. (Learning Management Systems)
- Simulations - Do it to learn it.
- Augmented Reality- Experience the learning
- Virtual Reality- Tours to far-flung areas
- Digital games and assessment tools
- PowerPoint presentations
- Students' videos and presentations
- Mobile Applications
- Collaborative assignments using cloud services like Google drive.
- Audio/Visual inputs

Digital Tools Used by Teachers for Assessment

- **Nearpod:** It is a website and app-based digital tool that enables teachers to create interactive slide-based learning resources for students to engage with and learn from. They can make lot of different interactive learning resources that allow students to engage and learn from their devices or a single screen in the room. It is also possible to add question points along the way and have the students participate as they go. Nearpod is also useful as a tool for formative assessment. It can output student efforts in charts in easy-to-analyse graphs and for a clear snapshot of progress. It can also use gamification to make learning engaging and fun. It is also made to work well with a lot of pre-existing tools, such as Google Slides, Microsoft PowerPoint, and YouTube. Teachers can easily take the help of media to make a lesson quickly and use existing resources.

- **Padlet:** It is a free and valuable education tool specifically created for teachers to organise, and share content, keeping it all in one place with virtual bulletin boards, which are called "padlets." This real-time collaborative web platform is the perfect tool for remote learning and can help increase participation and student engagement. It also creates a sense of community. It serves as an excellent exit slip to look for understanding, individual views, and creations.
- **Mentimeter:** It is an open digital application that allows students to continue learning in an engaging and interactive manner. It enables teachers to:
  - Engage with students using live polls, word clouds, quizzes, multiple-choice questions etc
  - Track learning and understanding by asking various questions and downloading results
  - Communicate and interact with students
  - Stay up-to-date with the syllabus so that no one misses anything thing.
  - Helps to plan assessment so that queries and questions can be discussed, explained and then clarified if needed.

FLIP Teaching

F.L.N. (FLIP Learning Network) describes Flipped Learning as a pedagogical approach wherein direct instruction moves from the group learning to individual learning. The resulting group space is transformed into a dynamic and interactive learning environment where the educator guides students as they apply concepts and engage in the subject matter.

To engage in Flipped Learning, teachers must ensure that they incorporate the four pillars into their practice that is, (F.L.I.P.) Flexible Environment, Learning Culture, Intentional Content and Professional Educator.

Four Pillars of FLIP Teaching

- **Flexible Environment:** Educators create spaces that are flexible, where students choose when and where they learn from. Additionally, such educators are flexible in their expectations of student timelines for learning and their assessments of student learning.
- **Learning Culture:** In a Flipped Learning model, during the in-class time, topics are explored, and rich learning opportunities are created. It makes students actively involved in knowledge construction as they get to participate in and self-

evaluate their learning in a personally meaningful manner.

- **Intentional Content:** Flipped Learning Educators decide what they need to teach and, at the same time, what materials students should handle independently. Educators make use of Intentional Content to maximise classroom time to adopt student-centred, active learning strategies, depending on the subject matter and grade level.

- **Professional Educator:** The function of a Professional Educator is even more critical and more demanding in a Flipped Classroom rather than in a traditional one. While teaching in the class, they need to observe students, provide them with instant feedback, and assess their work. While Professional Educators take on less prominent roles in a flipped classroom, they remain the essential part that enables Flipped Learning to function successfully.

The Flipped Learning model may not work for every kind of classroom set-up; the model represents an innovative and engaging approach to teaching with a high potential to create active, engaged and learning-centred classrooms. F.L.N.'s four suggested pillars serve as ways to help educators successfully implement the Flipped Learning model. ("*The Four Pillars of Flipped Learning*" by Mathew Lynch.)

Active Learning: Facilitation-Based Teaching

Teaching sometimes appears one way, with teachers pouring out their wisdom like a sage on a stage, while facilitation is more like a guide standing on the side to direct and support. Facilitation helps move a classroom culture towards Active Learning.

As described by Cornell University, active learning asks students to engage in their learning by thinking, discussing, investigating, and creating. In class, students practice skills, solve problems, make decisions, propose solutions, struggle with complex questions, and explain ideas in their own words through writing and discussion. Timely feedback from the instructor or fellow students is critical in this learning process. Education research shows that incorporating active learning strategies into university courses enhances student learning experiences significantly. (Freeman et al., 2014; Theobald et al., 2020).

Benefits of Active Learning

- It provides opportunities to process course material through thinking, writing, talking, and problem-solving, giving students multiple avenues for learning.

- Applying new knowledge helps students encode information, concepts, and skills in their memories by connecting them with prior notification, organising information, and strengthening neural pathways.

- Receiving frequent and immediate feedback helps students correct misconceptions and develop a deeper understanding of course material.
- Working on activities helps create personal connections with the material, which increases students' motivation to learn.
- Regular interaction with the instructor and peers around shared activities and goals helps create a sense of community in the classroom.
- Instructors may gain insight into student thinking by observing and talking with students as they work.
- Knowing how students understand the material helps instructors target their teaching in future lessons.

Getting Started with Active Learning Techniques

Whether you are thinking about trying active learning for the first time or have used it before and want to try something new, these are proven strategies for engaging students and focusing on key concepts in your class. Start with one and consider adding more as you become more comfortable. Breaking up your lesson every 15-20 minutes will help keep students' attention and interest as they apply what they are learning.

Tips To Keep in Mind as You Try New Techniques

- Use problems or questions that will challenge and interest your students
- Explain the purpose of the activity and be clear about what you want your students to do
- Allocate enough time for the activity; some in-class activities take only 2-3 minutes, but others may take longer.
- Break longer activities into stages or steps, so that students who finish early are not left waiting and students who need more help receive the feedback they need
- Leave time to debrief and identify the takeaways at the end of the activity to ensure that students receive feedback from you and/or their peers.

Though many people think of active learning as something that happens in the classroom, it is not often the case. Most active learning activities are paired with collaborative work outside of class.

Examples of Active Learning Paired with Collaborative Work Outside of Class

- **Write-Pair-Share:** Present students with a question, problem, or item for reflection. Have students reflect or write on their own for 1-2 minutes, then discuss with a peer for another 2 minutes. Call on several pairs to share their thoughts. Gauge student progress and provide further guidance if needed.

- **Minute Paper:** At a natural breaking point or the end of class, ask students to reflect on and write down 2 or 3 key points made in class. Another option is to ask them what they still do not understand (often called the "muddiest point") or if they have questions. Collect and review papers (in large classes, review a sample). Discuss student misconceptions or questions at the beginning of the next class. Alternatively, ask students to talk with their classmate(s) for feedback.

- **Catch Up:** Pause your lecture at a natural breaking point and give students a chance to catch up on their note-taking. Ask them to talk with a classmate about any points that are still unclear. Make time for 2 or 3 questions after the students discuss.

- **Brainstorming:** Ask students to talk in pairs or groups to develop a list of ideas in response to a question. Groups can volunteer their ideas as you compile a list to discuss.

- **Concept Mapping:** Ask your students to draw a concept map showing how the ideas you have been discussing relate to one another. Give students time to think on their own (or even prepare their maps prior to class) before asking them to discuss with others and modify. Students may need coaching on concept mapping before they begin. Share it using Post-it notes. It allows students to organise concepts. Expect to spend 10+ minutes on a mapping activity.

- **Drawing/ Diagrams (Idea 1):** Ask your students to draw and label from memory something they have been studying (e.g., an object, process etc.). Then ask them to work in pairs or groups to compare their drawings and discuss details they may have missed. Debrief by presenting and discussing an accurate representation. Give students time to add elements they have missed.

- **Drawing/ Diagrams (Idea 2):** Ask your students to draw a simplified design, plan, or process, then explain the rationale behind their choices to a peer. Students discuss and give feedback. To debrief, present your own or a student-created version and explain the critical elements. Allow time for questions. Depending on the complexity of the task, this activity may take more than 3 minutes. Idea 2, in particular, may take 7-10 minutes.

- **Writing Prompts:** Develop a prompt that asks your students to reflect on a topic or concept they have been studying in class. Prompts often ask students to apply their learning to their interests, current events, or real-world situations. You might ask your students to put themselves in the position of an expert who is advising a common man on an issue or need (for example, in their hometown). What advice would they give as an expert? Give your students time to think and write, then ask them to turn in their writing. Review and check for understanding. Depending on your prompt, this activity could take 3-10 minutes of the class time. It may be graded for participation or used as a way for you to check your student's understanding.

Cooperative Learning

As the name suggests, Cooperative Learning is an approach to learning where a group of students (ideally 04) work together to learn a new topic or completing a project. It has been proved highly effective for all types of learners, including mainstream students, academically gifted and language learners because it promotes learning, fosters respect, and strengthens friendships among diverse groups of students. In fact, the more diversity in a team, the higher the benefits for each student. Peers learn to depend on each other positively for various learning tasks.

Students ideally work in teams of four. This way, they can break into pairs for some activities and then get back together in teams very quickly again. It is important, however, to establish classroom ground rules or agreements and protocols that guide students to:

- Contribute
- Stay on task
- Help each other
- Encourage each other
- Share
- Solve problems
- Give and accept feedback from peers

Some popular strategies that can be used with all students to learn content (such as science, mathematics, social studies, language arts, and foreign languages) given by Kagan and observed over years are given below:

Strategies to Learn Content in The Classroom

- **Round Robin:** Present a category (such as "Names of Mammals") for discussion. Have students take turns going around the group and naming items that fit the category. (Kagan, 2009)
- **Roundtable:** Present a category (such as words that begin with "b"). Have students take turns writing one word at a time. (Kagan, 2009)
- **Write around:** For creative writing or summarization, give a sentence starter (for example: If you give an elephant a cookie, he's going to ask for...) Ask all students in each team to finish that sentence. Then, they pass their paper to the right, read the one they received, and add a sentence to that one. After a few rounds, four great stories or summaries emerge. Give children time to add a conclusion and/or

edit their favourite one to share with the class.

- **Numbered Heads Together:** Ask students to number off in their teams from one to four. Announce a question and a time limit. Students put their heads together to come up with an answer. Call a number and ask all students with that number to stand and answer the question. Recognise correct responses and elaborate through rich discussions. (Kagan, 2009)
- **Team Jigsaw:** Assign each student in a team one-fourth of a page to read from any text (for example, a social studies text) or one-fourth of a topic to investigate or memorise. Each student completes his or her assignment and then teaches the others or helps to put together a team product by contributing a piece of the puzzle.
- **Tea Party/Inner Circle-Outer Circle:** Students form two concentric circles or two lines facing each other. You ask a question (on any content), and students discuss the answer with the student facing them. After one minute, the outside circle or one line moves to the right so that students have new partners. Then pose a second question for them to discuss. Continue with five or more questions. For a bit of variation, students can write questions on cards to review for a test through this "Tea Party" method.

After every Cooperative Learning activity, you can debrief with the children by asking questions such as: What did you learn from this activity? How did you feel working with your teammates? If we do this again, how will you improve working together?

Peer Review: Teaching Students to Evaluate Each Other

Peer assessment can improve overall learning by helping students become better readers, writers, and collaborators. A well-designed and well-executed peer review program also develops students' evaluation and assessment skills. To implement the process of peer review following stages and steps can be considered:

Planning for Peer Review

- Identify where you can incorporate peer review exercises into your course.
- For peer review on written assignments, design guidelines that specify clearly defined tasks for the reviewer. Consider what feedback students can competently provide.
- Determine whether peer review activities will be conducted as in-class or out-of-class assignments (or as a combination of both).
- Plan for in-class peer reviews to last at least one class session. More time will be needed for longer papers and papers written in foreign languages.
- Model appropriate constructive criticism and descriptive feedback through the

comments you provide on papers and in class.

- Explain the reasons for peer review, its benefits, and how it supports course learning outcomes.
- Set clear expectations: determine whether students will receive grades on their contributions to peer review sessions. If grades are given, be clear about what you are assessing, what criteria will be used for grading, and how the peer review score will be incorporated into their overall course grade.

Before The First Peer Review Session

- Give students a sample paper to review and comment using the peer review guidelines. Ask students to share feedback and help them rephrase their comments to make them more specific and constructive, as needed.
- Consider using the sample paper exercise to teach students how to think about, respond to, and use comments by peer reviewers to improve their writing.
- Ask for input from students on the peer review worksheet or co-create a rubric in class.
- Prevent overly harsh peer criticism by instructing students to provide feedback as if they were speaking to the writer or presenter directly.
- Consider how you will assign students to groups. Do you want them to work together for the entire semester or change to different assignments? Do you want peer reviewers to remain anonymous? How many reviews will each assignment receive?

During & After Peer Review Sessions

- Give clear directions and time limits for in-class peer review sessions and set defined deadlines for out-of-class peer review assignments.
- Listen to group discussions and provide guidance and input when necessary.
- Consider requiring students to write a plan for revision indicating the changes they intend to make to the paper and explaining why they have chosen to acknowledge or disregard specific comments and suggestions. For exams and presentations, have students write about how they would approach the task next time based on the peer comments.
- Ask students to submit the peer feedback they received with their final papers. Make clear whether or not you will be taking this feedback into account when grading the paper or when assigning a participation grade to the student reviewer.
- Consider having students assess the quality of the feedback they received.
- Discuss the process in class, addressing problems that were encountered and what was learned.

Examples of Peer Review Activities

- After collection, redistribute papers randomly along with a grading rubric. After students have evaluated the papers, ask them to exchange them with a neighbour, evaluate the new paper, and then compare notes.
- After completing an exam, have students compare and discuss answers with a partner. You may offer them the opportunity to submit a new answer, dividing points between the two.
- In a small class, ask students to bring one copy of their paper with their name on it and one or two copies without a name. Collect the "name" copy and redistribute the others for peer review. Provide feedback on all student papers. Collect the peer reviews and return papers to their authors.
- Group presentations require the class to evaluate the group's performance using a predetermined marking scheme.
- When working on group projects, have students evaluate each group member's contribution to the project on a scale of 1-10. Require students to provide a rationale for how and why they are awarded points.

BEHAVIOURAL TRANSFORMATION

One of the biggest challenges of teachers dealing with large classes is classroom indiscipline. It is natural and global that students are always full of energy and never lose an opportunity to talk or make noise. We have seen teachers screaming out their lungs to make their students listen to them, but all goes in vain. It leaves the teacher frustrated and affects the quality of the lesson to be taught. There are certain ways that we have been using or have seen teachers using them to transform their classroom environment from chaos and tumult into order and receptivity. It has also been observed that classrooms that are dull and monotonous are more likely to fall into the trap of indiscipline and undesirable behaviour of children. Some of the effective and implementable approaches to bring behavioural transformation in the classroom are given below:

Energisers - Catalysts of Classroom Environment

Every classroom has energy; the higher the energy, the better the engagement. Teachers/facilitators use energisers at the beginning or middle of the session to infuse energy and vibrancy. Energising primarily involves movements, actions, dance, music, drawings, groupings and regroupings, swapping of places, and going outside the classroom for simple yet effective interventions like "Circle-Circle" or "Swap the place if..." etc.

The primary objective behind energisers is to change the classroom's energy and bring all the students or participants to almost the same level.

These quick energisers have proved to be an excellent approach to improving learners' attention span and retention ability. How often as students have you felt that some days the syllabus becomes too heavy and schools are not as attractive as they usually are? These cumbersome and stressful days when we wish there should have been some fun and joy not only after the regular periods but also intermittently in between the regular classroom periods.

Name Catch

Players: **8+** | Time: **10-15 minutes** | Equipment: **Ball**

Students sit in a big circle. A ball or other item is held by the Leader, who passes it to a player at random, saying first their own name, then the one to whom it was thrown, e.g., "Rishabh to Gurpreet". This player must immediately say their own name and then another player's name while passing it to that person. They must not pass it to their neighbour, nor can they pass it to someone they have passed to previously. This is a good, fun game to help people get to know the group members' names.

Tip: Play a piece of music with an obvious steady beat and see if players can pass the ball and say the names whilst keeping to the beat.

Blind Partnership

Players: **Pairs** | Time: **10-15 minutes** | Equipment: **Blindfolds**

In pairs, one person is blindfolded. Their partner must take them for a walk in a safe area, but one which has obstacles, such as tables, trees etc. The sighted person must guide the sightless one around the area using only speech – no bodily contact is allowed. As trust builds up, so should the pace – can any of the pair jog around the area?

What A Picture

Players: **Any** | Time: **15-30 minutes** | Equipment: **None**

Small groups are given a piece of paper with a scene written on it. They then have to organise themselves into a tableau of that scene – can other groups correctly identify the scene being portrayed? Suitable scenes could include a speech day, wedding, World Cup champions, a busy kitchen etc.

Remember The Circle

Ask the group to sit in a circle. Someone introduces themselves and says one thing they enjoy, for example, 'Hello! My name is Nicola, and I love to eat chocolate'. The person next to the facilitator goes next. They introduce themselves and say something that they enjoy or like doing. They then introduce themselves, for example, 'Hello! My name is Nombeko, and I love singing; this is Nicola, and she loves chocolate'. The game continues until each person is introduced. This game can be adapted to fit the theme of your workshop. For example, participants could introduce their name and a fact that they know about an issue/hope to change and so on.

Line Up

This energiser challenges everyone to cooperate in silence – they may use gestures. The group's task is to arrange themselves according to the month and day of their births. If they ask, "Where is the beginning of the line?" say that they'll have to figure that out in silence. When the movement ends, ask if they all feel comfortable with the arrangement. If not, they can continue. If they are comfortable, ask them to state the month and day of their births in order.

A variation is to ask people to line-up by height but do so with their eyes closed and humming all the time. When the movement ends, ask if they all feel comfortable with the arrangement. If not, they can continue for a while. Finally, have them open their eyes and see how they've done. When doing this with eyes closed, facilitators keep participants safe by redirecting them should they wander near the edge of the room or into furniture.

Zip Zap Zop

Standing in a circle, people place their palms together in front of them. The facilitator explains to the group that Zip Zap Zop all refer to different directions that they will point their hands.

- Zip: left
- Zap: right
- Zop: across the circle (or whatever you like).

Whoever starts has to choose one of Zip, Zop or Zop and say it out loud for example "Zip", and point his hands to the person on their left; it carries on (domino effect) with each person turning to the left with their hands and saying "Zip" until someone says something different such as "Zap" and then the direction changes to the right. It can just get faster or people who slip up sit down.

Blind Artist

One of our favourite games for students is definitely this one! Have your students form pairs. The students can't see each other. One student gets a drawing you prepared earlier. Ideally, the drawing should be something relevant to what you are teaching.

The student holding the drawing needs to give good instructions to the other student. The other students need to draw it without being able to see the original picture. If you want to spice up the classroom game, you can put a variety of conditions to it. For example, no asking questions or must draw with your non-writing hand etc. Aren't you curious about the results?

Statue/ Freeze

This simple technique has always helped me bring the noisy and chaotic class to a silent and still class for a few moments. It gives me the window to instruct students for the next activity. It is simple, like laying a ground rule at the beginning, that if the teacher says the word "Freeze" or "statue", students will freeze on the spot. Within a few seconds, the whole class comes to stand still, and the environment is ready to be steered by the teacher. It works well, especially with large-sized classrooms.

Give A Compliment

No one's too old for compliments! We all love it. This energiser makes students feel good about themselves by showering compliments. Each student gets a piece of paper taped on their back. Every student has to write a compliment on the paper that is on the back of every other student. They cannot miss a single one. Afterwards, the students can read their papers and all the compliments they have received.

Be Unique

This classroom game is about how unique one is and about different ways of getting to know each other better. Students form a circle. Every student is given a chance to say something unique about themselves. For example: "I have four cats." If another student also has four cats, the students who share the 'not-so-unique' aspect have to sit down. The goal is to stand till the end of the game and, therefore, to share only the very special things about yourself that no one else has got to share.

BRAIN BREAKS: ANSWERS TO DULL & MONOTONOUS CLASSROOMS

Brain breaks are an essential part of learning. They are designed to help students focus better and improve their retention power. They typically return students with renewed strength and allow blood and oxygen to flow to the brain. These breaks allow students a reset option during the day and enhance energy and relaxation. Examples include

Movement breaks, physical activities like stretches, yoga poses, jumping jacks, push-ups, or a quick dance party.

Strategies to Make Brain Breaks Work in the Classroom

- Let the kids know what you're doing.
- Plan according to your class schedule.
- Try different breaks for different brains.
- Identify when a brain break has started and ended.
- Do not be afraid to experiment.

How Do You Implement A Brain Break?

- Start the brain break. Set a timer and begin the break.
- Read the room. As students start their breaks, be prepared to provide support and adjust the brain break as necessary.
- Wrap up the break.
- Talk about the experience.

Examples of Two-Minute Brain Break Activities

- **Swap It:** Students stand in a circle, and if not possible, they can stand in their place. Call out a feature like "Everyone with curly hair", "Everyone whose name has more than 6 letters", "Everyone who had milk in the morning", etc. and everyone who has it swaps their positions. Students not having the trait will stay in their position.
- **Spot the Dice:** Mark six spots around the classroom and number them from 1 to 6. Instruct students to go to the spot of their choice. Now roll a numbered dice; the bigger the dice, the more fun. All the students at the number rolled go back to their seats. Students left then go to a new spot, and the dice is rolled again. The process continues until a few students are left.
- **Blindfold Dance Party!** A quick music and dance can prove to be a great brain break for students. Doing it blindfold makes the activity easier and much more fun for students. Students just love this break!
- **Dance-Freeze-Dance-** An extension/Variation to the blindfold dance party; here, in this activity, the music stops intermittently, and students freeze and hold their position until the music begins again.
- **Move it in my name:** Students stand behind their desks. Each student speaks out their name accompanied by a particular movement. For example- A student may say, "Karan" and roll his hands. The rest of the class says the name "Karan" and imitates the move. Then next student repeats the process, and so on.

- **Simon Says:** Simon Says is quite a famous activity that can transform the energy and the environment of any classroom. It is easy and great fun with a large class size. Here a teacher speaks, "Simon Says...." followed by an action to be performed, but if the action is spoken without the initial phrase, "Simon Says..." students must not perform the action. Creative teachers bring a lot of variations with Simon Says that make it an evergreen and ever-successful technique.

- **Movement Songs:** Some of the songs often played by teachers to energise the classroom environment are *"Bounce the Ball"*, *"Here We Go!"*; *"Let's Move!"*; *"Fruit Vendor"*, etc. *www.songsforteaching.com* is a website that aims to use music to promote learning and provides an extensive selection of songs that can be used with young learners.

- **Find It Fast:** Call out a colour or other trait (e.g. something round, something made of wood), and students must find an object in the room that fits the feature and get to it quickly.

- **Physical Challenges:** Challenge students to do something physically strenuous, such as standing on one foot with arms extended, or this one: Grab your nose with your left hand, grab your left earlobe with your right hand, and then quickly switch so that your right hand is on your nose. Your left hand is holding your right earlobe.

- **Plates:** Give each student a paper plate. Students must walk around the room, balancing the plates on their heads. If a student drops their plate, the student must freeze until another student picks it up and places it back on the student's head (while keeping their plate in place, of course).

- **Line Up!:** Have students line up using a specific criterion, such as age (use day and month, not just year), height, alphabetically by middle name, hair length, etc.

- **Floor is Lava:** This is a fun and active brain break that will get your kids moving and having a good time. You can play this either indoors or outdoors. The object of the activity is to have one person enter the room and yell, "floor is lava!" Everyone has five seconds to get their feet off the floor and whoever is still touching the floor loses.

- **Human Knot:** Divide students into groups of about eight students. Have students grab the right hand of someone not directly next to them. Then do the same with your left hand. The challenge is to untangle and become a circle without releasing hands.

- **Jump Skip Counting:** Have students count by twos, fives, tens etc., while jumping with each count. You could also practice spelling words this way.

- **Brain Yoga:** Have students hold their left ear with their right hand and nose with their left hand and then swap hands. Let them repeat the actions and see the whole class being charged with laughter and smiles.

All these ideas and strategies mentioned in the chapter emerge out of the needs or imagination. As an experienced and trained teacher, you can critically analyse the needs of your lessons and learners and devise ways and opportunities to use these transformative interventions. Modify them according to your resources and classroom demographics. If the need arises, think of new ideas to transform the classroom environment. More lively and interactive classrooms are real-time indicators of the overall high happiness index of the classroom.

Keep your mindset positive, optimistic and progressive so that you may explore, expand, and extract opportunities to make your classroom atmosphere more connected, conducive, and communicative for a joyful and productive classroom.

EPILOGUE

S miling Chalk is a subconscious message for teachers to realise the need for creating classrooms where everyone and everything is happy. Here teachers feel honoured to teach, and learners take pride in learning. Here chalks are delighted to be a medium to disseminate knowledge, and dusters are glad to make the platform ready for the knowledge to be transferred. The book's core idea emerges from a simple realisation that "Happy Teachers Create Classrooms, and Happy Classrooms are the foundational blocks of a Happy Nation".

This book may serve as a guide for those who aspire to use the tools and techniques, and an idea incubator for those who wish to ideate new tools for creating happy classrooms. This book results from our first-hand experiences with teaching, mentoring, observing and training.

We envision a classroom with laughter, celebrations, achievements, and transformations. We believe in the immense power of a teacher who can shape an individual's future, thus, society at large. With great powers comes great responsibility, and it is true vice versa. Shaping an individual's future is a great responsibility; thus, it comes with extraordinary abilities like the power of influencing, explaining, connecting, and transforming.

As teachers, you must look for ways and ideas to make your classrooms happy and valued learners. Your continuous professional development is equally important as the learning of your pupils. Stay hungry to learn more and willing to bring your learnings into action. Your professional growth is not measured by your designation or pay scales but by the ability to transform yourself, your classrooms, and your learners. The pass percentage of your class does not measure your impact but the inspired faces of your learners. You leave deep impressions on your learners' minds; make sure you leave inspiring, encouraging, and loving impressions.

This book will serve its true purpose the day you use any suggested ideas and experience true joy among your children.

"Sow the seeds of joyful teaching to reap the fruits of joyful learning"

HAPPINESS,
ENGAGEMENT,
AWARENESS,
RESOURCES &
TRANSFORMATION

BIBLIOGRAPHY

1. https://www.labhya.org/impact

2. https://en.wikipedia.org/wiki/Happiness_Curriculum

3. https://indianexpress.com/article/education/happiness-curriculum-is-a-massive-success-sisodia-7489100/

4. https://www.takingcharge.csh.umn.edu/what-mindfulness

5. https://happinessdelhi.blogspot.com/2020/02/session-2-mindful-listening.html

6. https://www.eastmojo.com/news/2020/08/24/meghalaya-teacher-wins-national-award-know-the-untold-story/

7. https://blog.skolera.com/how-to-handle-disengaged-students/

8. https://www.goodreads.com/book/show/23398899-creative-schools

9. https://onlineprograms.smumn.edu/mase/masters-in-special-education/resources/lesson-plans-learning-disabilities

10. https://7mindsets.com/student-engagement-strategies/

11. https://www.chalk.com/resources/gamification-in-the-classroom-how-to-get-started/

12. https://www.classpoint.io/4-classroom-gamification-examples/

13. https://teaching.cornell.edu/resource/examples-collaborative-learning-or-group-work-activities

14. https://americanenglish.state.gov/resources/teachers-corner-building-autonomy-and-independence-young-learners

15. https://www.tesol.org/docs/default-source/books/6P/6p-quickvisualguide_web.pdf?sfvrsn=0

16. https://americanenglish.state.gov/files/ae/resource_files/have_you_ever_instructions.pdf

17. https://americanenglish.state.gov/files/ae/resource_files/about_me_instructions_0.pdf

18. https://eric.ed.gov/?q=source%3a%22international+online+journal+of+primary+education&pg=1440&id=EJ1065471

19. https://lessons.myjli.com/communication/index.php/lesson-2/become-a-better-listener-active-listening/

20. https://assets.gov.ie/41319/6979e81cdfe44082a9faa4a11db99d5b.pdf

BIBLIOGRAPHY

21. https://americanenglish.state.gov/resources/teachers-corner-classroom-management

22. https://dz.usembassy.gov/education-culture/exchanges/

23. https://www.tesol.org/docs/books/bk_morethannative_325

24. https://www.studocu.com/ph/document/cebu-technological-university/bachelor-in-elementary-education/lesson-6-models-of-instruction/24143531

25. https://www.weareteachers.com/graphic-organizers/

26. https://dpi.wi.gov/sites/default/files/imce/ela/bank/6-12_L.VAU_Frayer_Model.pdf

27. https://adayinourshoes.com/what-is-frayer-model/

28. https://www.teacherspayteachers.com/Product/Star-of-the-Week-or-Day-4781783

29. https://www.weareteachers.com/exit-tickets/

30. https://venngage.com/blog/performance-review-examples/

31. https://www.ehyde.com/No%20Hands/

32. https://www.theedadvocate.org/the-four-pillars-of-flipped-learning/

33. https://teaching.cornell.edu/teaching-resources/active-collaborative-learning/active-learning

34. https://teaching.cornell.edu/getting-started-active-learning-techniques

35. https://www.colorincolorado.org/article/cooperative-learning-strategies

36. https://teaching.cornell.edu/resource/teaching-students-evaluate-each-other

37. https://www.dofe.org/thelatest/teambuilding-games/

38. https://commonslibrary.org/games-and-energisers/

39. https://www.bookwidgets.com/blog/2016/10/15-fun-classroom-energizers-for-students

40. https://www.healthgrades.com/right-care/angioplasty/benefits-and-risks-of-a-heart-stent

41. https://minds-in-bloom.com/20-three-minute-brain-breaks/

42. https://www.girlsaskguys.com/other/q1215907-would-you-rather-be-able-to-talk-with-animals-or-be-able-to-speak-all

43. https://www.lifehack.org/900271/brain-breaks-for-kids

44. https://www.self.com/gallery/best-shoulder-exercises

ABOUT THE AUTHORS

Karamjeet Singh   **Aditi Bhasin**

Mr. Karamjeet Singh and **Ms. Aditi Bhasin**, both these educators and authors have a rich and diversified experience of more than 2 decades. Being teacher and mentor with the Directorate of Education Delhi they had an opportunity to visit exemplary schools and institutions both nationally and internationally. It was through such experiences and exposures that they realised the siginificance of happy classrooms and gather key ideas to transform the classroom environment.

They have developed trainings and modules for Pre service and in service teachers on topics dealing with stress, positive mental attitude, effective communication, classroom management, peer observations etc. For learners, they have co-authored several books for SCERT and DoE (Delhi) like English Grammar Workbook, Pragati series, English Foundation Material, Language Games for Elementary students etc. Being Mentor teachers since 2016, i.e. the beginning of the mentorship programme, they have been involved in the flagship programmes of Delhi Government like *Mission Buniyad*, *the Happiness Curriculum*, *Entrepreneurship Mindset Curriculum*, and *Deshbhakti curriculum* etc.

They have received professional development trainings from world class institutions like NIE (Singapore), TESOL, US Embassy, NCERT and Arizona State University. The learnings assisted them to design, develop and deliver workshops for teachers on various topics for enhancing classroom engagement. Their enthusiasm to share their learnings through innumerable experiences have made them the Key Resource Person for SCERT trainings and have been recognised and awarded for their innovative Teaching Learning Materials. They have been officially invited by TESOL for their international conference as a presenter.

They strongly believe that, "*Happy Teachers Create Happy Classrooms*" thus they find passion in creating and compiling tools and strategies for making teachers, learners and classrooms happy.

Presently, Karamjeet is working as an Academic Coordinator and Lecturer English at one of the Government schools of Delhi and Aditi has been given the charge of special duties that includes planning and coordinating effective trainings for a large team of Mentor teachers and Academic Coordinators.